PAN-ISLAM

PAN-ISLAM

BY

G. WYMAN BURY

GYAN

Published by

Gyan Publishing House
5, Ansari Road
Daryaganj, New Delhi-110002
Phone: 011-47034999, 9811692060
E-mail: books@gyanbooks.com

Distribution Network

gyanbooks.com

India, USA, Canada, UK, Australia, France

ISBN: 978-81-212-7109-7 (PB)
First Published, 1919

2nd Impression 2024

Printed at: Gyan Press, Delhi.

PAN-ISLAM
Author: G. WYMAN BURY

PAN-ISLAM

PAN-ISLAM

BY

G. WYMAN BURY

Author of "The Land of Uz," "Arabia Infelix."

MACMILLAN AND CO., LIMITED
ST. MARTIN'S STREET, LONDON
1919

TO

MY WIFE

PREFACE

I HAVE written this book to present the main factors of a many-sided problem—political, social and religious—in a form which the general public can easily grasp.

Modern democratic principles tend to give the public increasing control of international and inter-racial affairs, and therefore any contribution to public knowledge on such questions is in the interests of sound administration.

The book is not intended to advise those who actually handle these affairs : I give such advice, when required, in more detail and not through the medium of a published work.

" Pan-Islam " is an elementary handbook, not a text-book—still less an exhaustive treatise, but the questions it discusses are real enough. My qualifications for writing it are based on a quarter of a century's experience of the subject in most parts of the Moslem world, and I have studied the question in areas which I have not actually visited through intercourse with pilgrims from those parts.

I have no axe to grind or infallible panacea to advocate; I merely lay the result of my researches before the public for its information, as failing health has warned me to "pass the ball when collared," and I would like to think that the land where most of my life's work has centred will not be mishandled by cranks and opportunists after I have left the game.

An arm-chair is a sorry substitute for an Arab pony, and a garden plot for the highlands of Arabia Felix, but the human mind is not necessarily confined by such trammels, and if my environment is narrow I hope my book is not.

G. Wyman Bury.

Helouan, 27th July, 1919.

CONTENTS

CHAPTER I

PAGE

ITS ORIGIN AND MEANING 11

CHAPTER II

ITS BEARING ON THE WAR 24

CHAPTER III

ITS STRENGTH AND WEAKNESS 83

CHAPTER IV

MOSLEM AND MISSIONARY 110

CHAPTER V

A PLEA FOR TOLERANCE 187

PAN-ISLAM

CHAPTER I

ITS ORIGIN AND MEANING

MUCH has been written about Christianity and Islam, so I hasten to inform my readers that this is not a religious treatise, nor do I class them with the globe-trotter who searched Benares brass-bazar diligently for "a really nice image of Allah" and pronounced the dread name of Hindustan's avenging goddess like an effervescing drink.

I presuppose that Christians or Moslems who read this book have got beyond the stage of calling each other pagans or *kafirs*, and it will have served its purpose if it brings about a friendlier feeling between the two great militant creeds whose adherents have confronted together many a stricken field.

Most people have heard of the pan-Islamic movement, especially during the War. Some for their art, learning, or handicraft when we were massacring Jews in London as part of a coronation pageant.

Medieval Moslems never fanned the movement into flame as long as they were let alone, and even now tribes living beyond the scope of missionaries and traders prefer the Christian traveller whom they know to the Moslem stranger from the coast whom they usually distrust, and who, to do him justice, seldom ventures among them, unless compelled by paramount self-interest, generally in connection with some European scheme or other.

Hitherto pan-Islam had been an instinctive and entirely natural *riposte* to the menace or actual aggression of non-Moslems; it assumed the character of a definite organisation under the crafty touch of that wily diplomat Abdul Hamid, once called by harsh critics "the Damned," though his efforts in that direction have been quite eclipsed by more recent exponents.

In extreme evangelical circles it used to be frequently urged that pan-Islam was a bugbear discovered, if not created, by one of India's most eminent Viceroys, whose remarks thereon are said to have given Abdul Hamid the hint. This method of eliminating a danger by denying its existence has been discredited, since 1914, as completely as the somewhat similar one (attributed to Mississippi engineers) of sitting on the safety-valve just too long for safety. Moreover, in view of Abdul's undoubted ability, he probably discovered for himself its efficacy as a weapon of reprisal when hard pressed by pertinacious and inquisitive Ambassadors, for he often found himself much embarrassed in his dealings with Armenia and other domestic affairs by the intrusions of the more formidable Christian Powers.

Great Britain naturally felt the point of this weapon most as governing wide Moslem territories, and one can imagine some such interview as this:

"Frontier rectifications, my dear Sir Nicholas? By all means—and, talking about frontiers, I do hope affairs are quite quiet now on your north-west frontier; I take such an interest in my East Indian correspondence."

And those Britons who have handled Oriental affairs for the last twenty years can appreciate the extent of that interest when we remember that even while Yamen Arabs were fighting the Turks, their neighbours on the Aden side of the frontier were praying in their mosques that the Sultan and his troops might be victorious "by land and sea."

All this, however, was merely playing with

intrigue as a political counterpoise; it remained for a Christian nation to put pan-Islam on a business footing. First we have polite bagmen calling at Stamboul with German guns and a German military system. Then "our Mr. William" of the well-known Potsdam firm of Hohenzollern and Sons made his great advertising campaign in the Near East; many of us remembered his theatrical visit to Saladin's tomb and the tawdry wreath with its bombastic inscription, "From the Emperor of the Franks to the Emperor of the Saracens—Greeting."

That astute "pilgrim" made himself especially affable to the American Protestant missionaries in the Holy Land, preached to a small but select congregation at the church of the Holy Sepulchre, and posed alternately as a pious but militant Moslem (when Hajji Guiyaum rode in military pomp into Jerusalem) and as a prince of peace. That the hospice of Kaiserin Augusta Victoria on the top of the Mount of Olives was loopholed for musketry and mounted a searchlight in its tower that could signal with Haifa was possibly due to some wayward caprice of the builder, but it came in very useful later on. So did the scholarly researches of eminent Germans in Sinai, assisted as they were by maps which the Anglo-Egyptian authorities courteously placed at their disposal, and which formed a basis for a more detailed survey of wells and routes.

But the old firm at Potsdam excelled itself in its representatives on the Palestine coast. There was, for example, the German Consul at Haifa famed for his culture and diplomacy (the Teutonic brand), who also spoke Arabic, Turkish, French and English fluently. This gifted official frequented native cafés, where he fraternised with the local Arabs and conducted a vigorous verbal propaganda against the Entente. Then there was the German engineer who wrecked the British railway scheme to connect Haifa and Damascus and re-naturalised as a German citizen after being American Consul. The Belgian Vice-Consul too, that merry Hun, who was also agent for our Khedivial mail line. When the Turks came in against us this good and faithful servant danced on the Belgian and British flags and threw himself heart and soul into pan-Islamic propaganda.

Nor must we overlook that reverend pastor and Koranic scholar who distributed anti-Christian and more especially anti-British propaganda by means of native emissaries. Last but not least, the Herr Direktor of the Hejaz Railway, who was collecting railway material for Sinai before war broke out. Some time before the Turks came in he imported, for the alleged use of the Jewish technical school, so great a quantity of high explosives that it caused a panic in Haifa. Yet it did not sufficiently impress our Levantine Vice-Consul there for him to report it, though the German Consul's remarkable activity to get the stuff landed might have given him the hint.

At Jeddah our Khedivial Mail Agency, under the good old English name of Robinson, was a perfect nest of Germans and pro-German Dutchmen when I called there in 1912. They were very active early in the War, but had wisely disappeared before my last visit, when Jeddah fell to our blockade and bombardment.

As for Hodeidah, the chief port of Yamen, it was the happy hunting-ground of a great German firm, and the American Consul was himself a German.

Decidedly, for people who believed that they had a monopoly of Divine assistance, they had taken a lot of pains that their Holy War should be a success.

To grasp the world-wide conspiracy which hatched out so many formidable events during the War and to appreciate the causes which contributed to its final collapse we must take a comprehensive glance at the Ottoman Caliphate and how it came about.

Remember, the Ottoman Turks are not Semitic,

as is the bulk of the Moslem world. Tradition derives them from Turk, son of Japhet, and they are a Turco-Mongol blend which most people agree to call Tartar. Their language is closely allied to Mongolian, though written in Arabic, or rather Persian, character, and its Arabic words are pronounced unintelligibly to an Arab. A true Turk learns Arabic with difficulty, and a far higher percentage of Britons in India speak Hindustani than Turks do Arabic in Turkish Arabia.

Then, again, look at their early history. Their Mongol-Turkish ancestors were driven westward because they made Mongolia too hot for them, and we hear of Turks smelting iron for their Mongol masters in what is now Eastern Turkestan until they threw off the Mongol yoke in A.D. 552, when Turkish history begins.

At the dawn of Islam (A.D. 632) Turks and Mongols were harrying each other all over the Caspian countries like rival wolf-packs, sometimes combining for a raid on their neighbours and then fighting over the loot. That is why you find racial Turks in such outlandish places as Merv, Khiva, Samarcand, Bokhara and Cabul, for the Turkish race is not confined to Asia Minor and Turkey in Europe, but is scattered over parts of Russia and China and Afghanistan.

Now to consider the Ottoman Turks, with whom we are chiefly concerned. They were superior to their Mongol fellow-wolves in that they could smelt iron and had some idea of constructive enterprise. They had also adopted Islam, which was a great advance from the Shamanistic wizardry and totem-worship they used to practise, and their contact with the Arabs who raided them and afterwards accepted their military service to the Caliphate had civilised them considerably. Their Seljouk cousins were already ruling in Asia Minor, whither they had been driven by the Mongols when a wandering Turkish band sought similar asylum there in the earlier part of the thirteenth century and intervened most opportunely to help the Seljouks repulse a Mongol raid; in return, the Seljouk Emperor gave them a grant of land in Bithynia.

In 1300 the Seljouk Empire was finally smashed by the Mongols, who withdrew eastward without occupying the country, for they were merely predatory and destructive and had no gift or desire for permanent colonisation. So it came about that the Ottoman Empire began in 1326 under Othman I in Bithynia and grew by absorption and lack of effective opposition until, in 1517, we find it spreading under Selim I (the

Magnificent) to the gates of Vienna and extending from Germany to Persia and from Arabia to the Atlantic.

The benign sun of the Arabian Caliphate, under which learning and industry flourished securely, had long since set in blood under circumstances of treachery and murder which have hardly been surpassed even in the late war.

Under the later Abbasides, when the glories of the Caliphate were waning, there were bitter dissensions between Sunnis and Shiahs (the main orthodox and schismatic sects of Islam) which culminated in fierce rioting at Baghdad in 1258. The then Caliph was foolish enough to appeal for assistance against the schismatic seditionists to his Mongol neighbours. It had been done before under similar conditions, and even in these days such a manœuvre seems still to appeal to some types of religious fanaticism, judging by certain passages between our sister isle and the modern Hun. On the above occasion, however, it was practised once too often. Hulaku Khan, the fierce Mongol chief, had long had his eye on Baghdad as holding princely loot in all too slack a grip, for the Caliphate had been relying on Tartar mercenaries for years.

He approached that queen of cities, as she then was, with a great host, lured the Caliph out to meet him by the promise of an alliance, and murdered the whole party, the Caliph being trampled to death. Then Baghdad was given over to sack and massacre for more than a month, by which time 1,800,000 people are said to have perished.

The Caliphate was transplanted to Cairo, where it dragged out an anæmic existence until Selim I seized it, with the person of the then Caliph, by right of conquest, and it has been an appanage of the Ottoman reigning house ever since.

Selim the Magnificent may be called the Turkish top-note. After him the Ottoman Empire gradually declined. It has generally taken advantage of disaster or dissension to extend its borders—a precarious method of empire-building unless consolidated by benevolent and sound administration, which is not a feature of Turkish rule. Add to this the facts that Turks are slack Moslems, that the national party which ousted Abdul Hamid (himself most orthodox) is not religious at all, with all its barbarian, totemistic nonsense of the "White Wolf," and that they *would* pose as conquerors on insufficient grounds, and we begin to see why they have been kicked out of their Asiatic empire bit by bit.

If Turk and Mongol had been capable of dynastic

evolution and co-ordinate policy they might have shared most of the Eastern Hemisphere between them. We have seen the high-water mark of the Ottoman Empire; Marco Polo has told us of Kubla Khan's Chinese Empire, and the Moguls did much for India in their prime. But the wolf-taint was in their blood, and just as a pet wolf gets fat and degenerate, so it has been with these Tartars. Their undoubted soldierly qualities are sapped by luxury, and they possess no constructive gifts which peace and prosperity might develop. Hence it is that every empire they have founded has risen to a culminating point of conquest and then dwindled away in sloth and corruption.

The Turk is not fit to be put in charge of any race but his own, for he is at heart a bitter wolf who will turn and rend without ruth or warning. I have met Turks who have shown tact, humanity, and ability under trying conditions, and I have met well-mannered wolves in captivity, but would not trust the pack ranging in its native forest. I once heard a member of our Ottoman Embassy who has unique experience of the Turk size him up as follows: "The Turk can be a suave and cultured gentleman till his time comes, and then he will tear your guts out and *dance* on them." It was the Seljouk Turks whose persecutions caused the Crusades. Before them, Arab rule in Palestine was tolerant enough, and the Caliph Omar was scrupulously careful when he entered Jerusalem as a conqueror to respect Christian prejudices and the monuments of our creed.

So it came about that their empire was dropping from them piecemeal even before the War, for a race that can no longer conquer and has never learned to conciliate must draw in its borders or cease to exist as a State.

When war broke out Turkey was just hanging on to the last scrap of her empire in Europe and had lost all but the shadow of sovereignty in Egypt, while Arabia was seething with discontent, where not in actual revolt, and regarded the belated efforts of local officials to govern tactfully as signs of weakness.

The colossal brigandage of Germany appealed to her freebooting instincts, although it took a corrupt, self-seeking Government and a final push from the "Goeben" and the "Breslau" to plunge her into war against her best friends.

To proclaim a *jihad* was her obvious course, if only to keep Arabia moderately quiet, apart from its value as a weapon against her Christian foes. We will now see how she fared in the "Holy War."

CHAPTER II

ITS BEARING ON THE WAR

QUITE early in the War those of us who had to deal with pan-Islamic propaganda realised that the widespread organisation which Germany had grafted on to the original Turkish movement must have existed some time before the outbreak of actual hostilities.

For example, there was a snug, smooth-running concern at San Francisco which spread its tentacles all over the Moslem world, but specialised in a seditious newspaper called *El'-Ghadr*, which means treachery or mutiny. This was particularly directed at our Indian Army, but Egypt was not forgotten. A gifted censor sent us an early copy, but had, unfortunately, lost the wrapper, so our earnest desire to make the addressee's closer acquaintance was thwarted.

Stamboul was naturally an active centre, and, before the Turks entered the War, Turkish officers in full uniform, and sometimes even wearing swords, permeated Cairo cafés with espionage and verbal propaganda, trying to fan into flame the military ardour of Egyptian students and men about town. This last activity was wasted effort, as anyone who knew the type could have told them; the effendis abstained from the crudities of personal service and confined themselves to stirring up the town riffraff, who wanted a safer form of villainy than open riot, and the *fellahin*, who wanted a safe market for their produce and easy taxation, both of which they stood to lose by violence. Many a *fellah* still believes that the War was a myth created by the authorities to put prices up. Even Teuton activity failed to stimulate these placid folk, and the glad tidings preached by the madder type of German missionary that the Kaiser was the Messiah left them unmoved.

When the Turks came in against us, and the ex-Khedive, safe among his new-found friends, threw off the mask, the Cairene effendis became tremendously active. Forgetting how they had disliked Abbas II and called him a huckstering profligate, they mourned for his deposal by wearing black ties, especially the students. Some of these enthusiastic young heroes even went so far as to scatter chlorate of potash crackers about when their school was visited by poor old Sultan

Husein (who was worth six of his predecessor), and he got quite a shock, which was flagrantly and noisomely accentuated by asafœtida bomblets.

The ex-Khedive did not share their patriotic grief. He was quite comfortable while awaiting the downfall of British rule, for, with shrewd prescience that almost seems inspired, he had taken prudent measures for his future comfort and luxury before leaving Egypt on his usual summer tour to Europe. He had mortgaged real estate up to the hilt, realised on immobile property as far as possible, and diverted his fluid assets through various channels beyond the reach of his sorrowing subjects and the Egyptian Government. When an official inventory was taken in Abdin Palace at the accession of the late Sultan Husein, it was ascertained that the famous inlaid and begemmed coffee-service, which, like our Crown jewels, was not supposed to leave the country, had been sent after the ex-Khedive to his new address—truly a man of parts. I have often wondered whether his Hunnish friends got him to disgorge by means of a forced loan or war-bonds, or something of that sort. If so, they achieved something notable, for he has left behind him, beside his liabilities, the name of being a difficult man to get money out of.

When the Turco-Teuton blade was actually drawn in Holy War I was down with enteric, which I had contracted while working in disguise among seditious circles in the slums of Old Cairo. I just convalesced in time to join the Intelligence Staff on the Canal the day before Jemal Pasha's army attacked. His German staff had everything provided for in advance with their usual thoroughness. From the documents and prisoners that came through our hands we learnt that the hotel in Cairo where the victors were to dine after their triumphant entry had actually been selected, and some enthusiasts went so far as to insist that the menu had been prepared. If so, they omitted to get the Canal Army on toast, and for want of this indispensable item the event fell through. All the same, it was a soldierly enterprise, and if the Senussis had invaded in force or the population risen behind us, as they hoped would be the case, the result might have been different.

As it was they put up a very good fight and their arrangements for getting across the Sinaitic desert were excellent. For the last ten miles they man-handled their pontoons to the edge of the Canal. These craft were marvels of lightness and carrying capacity, but, of course, no protection whatever against even a rifle-bullet, and they had not fully reckoned with the Franco-British naval flotilla, which proved a formidable factor.

The morning after the main fight a little Syrian subaltern passed through my hands. He had been slightly wounded in the leg and still showed signs of nervous shock, so I made him sit down with a cigarette while I questioned him. He had been in charge of a pontoon manned by his party and said that they had got halfway across the Canal in perfect silence when "the mouth of hell opened" and the pontoon was sinking in a swirl of stricken men amid a hail of projectiles. He and two others swam to our side of the Canal, where they surrendered to an Indian detachment.

Our Indian troops on the Canal were naturally a mark for pan-Islamic propaganda reinforced by Hindu literature of the *Bande Mataram* type—a double-barrelled enterprise to bag both the great creeds of India. The astute propagandists had a pamphlet or two aimed at Sikhism, which they seemed to consider a nation, as they spoke of their national aspirations, though an elementary study of the subject might have taught them that it was a religious and secular movement originally intended to curb Moslem power in India during the sway of the later Moguls. Anyone but a Moslem can be a Sikh.

Naturally I was on the *qui vive* for signs of pan-Islamic activity on the enemy's side, and I questioned my little Syrian very closely to ascertain how far the movement was used as a driving force among the troops engaged against us. He, personally, had rather a grievance on the subject, for the Indian Moslems who took him had reproached him bitterly for fighting on the wrong side. "I fought," he said, "because it was my duty as an officer of the Ottoman Army. I know that men were invited to join as for a *jihad*, but we officers did not deceive ourselves. *Par exemple*, I think myself a better Moslem than any Turk, but what would you?" I consoled the little man while concealing my satisfaction at the feeling displayed against him. An extraordinarily heterogeneous collection of prisoners came dribbling through my hands directly after the Turks were repulsed. Most were practically deserters who had been forcibly enrolled, given a Mauser and a bandoleer, and told to go and fight for the Holy Places of Islam. As one of the more intelligent remarked, "If the Holy Places are really in danger, what are we doing down this way?"

They came from all over the Moslem world. There were one or two Russian pilgrims returning from Mecca to be snapped up by the military authorities at Damascus railway station when they got out of the pilgrim train from Medina. There were cabdrivers from Jerusalem, a stranded pilgrim from China, several Tripolitans who had been roped in on the Palestine seaboard while trying to get a passage home, a Moor who tried to embrace my feet when I spoke of the snow-crowned Atlas above Morocco City (Marraksh) and told him that he would be landed at Tangier in due course—Inshallah. Of course we released, and repatriated as far as we could, men who were not Ottoman subjects and had obviously been forced into service against us. A few days later, when Jemal Pasha's army was getting into commissariat difficulties out in the Sinaitic desert (for the Staff had relied on entering Egypt), we began to get the real Turks among our prisoners.

I was very curious to ascertain if they had been worked up with pan-Islamic propaganda or carried any of it on them, for there was not even a Red Crescent Koran on any of the Arabic-speaking prisoners. A search of their effects revealed a remarkable phase of propaganda. There was hardly any religious literature except a loose page or two of some pious work like the "Traditions of Muhammad," but there were quantities of rather crude (and very lewd) picture-cards portraying soldiers in Turkish uniform outraging and murdering nude or semi-nude women and children, while corpses in priestly garb, shattered crucifixes, and burning churches indicated the creed that was being so harried and gave the scene a stimulating background. From their appearance I should say these pictures were originally engraved to commemorate Balkan or Armenian atrocities, but their possessors, on being closely questioned, admitted that the impression conveyed to them was of the joyous licence which was to be theirs among the Frankish civilians after forcing the Canal. One Kurdish gentleman had among his kit fancy socks, knitted craftily in several vivid colours, also ornate slippers to wear in his promised palatial billet at Cairo. There were some odd articles among the kit of these Turkish prisoners, to wit, a brand-new garden thermometer, which some wag insisted was for testing the temperature of the Canal before immersion, and a lavatory towel looted from the Hejaz railway. Still, nothing was quite so remarkable as a white flag with a jointed staff in a neat, compact case which had been carried by a German officer. Among his papers was an indecent post-card not connected, I think, with propaganda of any sort, as it portrayed a bright-coloured female of ripe figure and

Teutonic aspect, wearing a pair of long stockings and high-heeled shoes, and bore the legend "Gruss von München."

A certain coyness, or possibly an appreciation of their personal value, kept most of the German officers from actual contact with our line. Only one reached the Canal bank, and he is there still. The German touch, however, was much in evidence. There were detailed written orders about manning the pontoons, not to talk, cough, sneeze, etc., and for each man to move along the craft as far as feasible and then sit down. They seem to have relied entirely on surprise, and ignored the chance of its occurring on the wrong side of the Canal. The emergency rations too which we found on the earlier batches of prisoners had a distinctly Teutonic flavour—they were so scientifically nourishing in theory and so vilely inedible in practice. They were a species of flat gluten cake rather like a dog-biscuit, but much harder. An amateur explosive expert of ours tested one of these things by attempting detonation and ignition before he would let his batch of prisoners retain them, which, to do their intelligence justice, they were not keen on doing, but offered any quantity of the stuff for cigarettes. We ascertained from them that you were supposed to soak it in water before tackling it in earnest, but as the only supply (except the runlet they still carried on them) was in the fresh-water canal behind our unshaken line, such a course was not practicable; the discovery of a very dead Turk some days later in that canal led to the ribald suggestion that he had rashly endeavoured to eat his ration. Our scientist laid great stress on its extraordinary nutritive properties, but desisted, after breaking a tooth off his denture, in actual experiment.

German influence, too, was apparent in the relations between officers and men. A Turkish *yuzbashi* was asked to get a big batch of prisoners to form two groups according to the languages they spoke—Arabic or Turkish. It was not an easy task in the open on a pitch-black night, but he did it with soldierly promptitude and flung his glowing cigarette end in the face of a dilatory private. As a natural corollary it may be mentioned here that one or two of our prisoners had deserted after shooting officers who had struck them.

For some days after the battles of Serapeum and Toussoum we expected another attempt, but they had been more heavily mauled than we thought at first. The dead in the Canal were kept down by the weight of their ammunition for some time, and the shifting sand on the

Sinaitic side was always revealing hastily-buried corpses on their line of retreat.

Jemal Pasha hurried back to Gaza and published a grandiloquent report for Moslem consumption, to the effect that the Turks were already in Cairo (as was indeed the case with many hundreds), and that, of the *giaour* fleet, one ship had sunk, one had been set on fire, and the rest had fled. Two heavy howitzers, as a matter of fact, had managed by indirect fire from a concealed position to land a couple of projectiles on the "Hardinge," which was not originally built for such rough treatment, being an Indian marine vessel taken over by the Navy. She gave more than she got when her four-point-sevens found the massed Turkish supports.

A great deal of criticism has been flung at this first series of fights on the Canal, mostly by Anglo-Egyptian civilians. They asked derisively whether we were protecting the Canal or the Canal us. The answer is in the affirmative to both questions. Ordinary steamer traffic was only suspended for a day during the first onslaught, and the G.O.C. was not such a fool as to leave the Canal in his rear and forgo the defensive advantage. There are some who, in their military ardour, would have had him pursue the enemy into the desert, forgetting that to leave a sound position and pursue a superior force on an ever-widening front in a barren country which they know better than you do and have furnished with their own supply-bases is just asking for trouble. Our few aeroplanes in those days could only reconnoitre twenty miles out, and there was no evidence that the enemy had not merely fallen back to his line of wells preparatory to another attempt. We had not then the men, material, or resources for a triumphant advance into Sinai; it was enough to make sure of keeping the enemy that side of the Canal with the Senussi sitting on the fence and Egypt honeycombed with seditious propaganda.

Anyone at all in touch with native life in Cairo could gauge the extent of propagandist activity by gossip at cafés and in the bazars. The Senussi was marching against us. India was in revolt and the Indian Army on the Canal had joined the Turks. The crowning stroke of ingenuity was a tale that received wide credence among quite intelligent Egyptians. It was to the effect that the Turks had commandeered an enormous number of camels and empty kerosene tins. This was quite true so far, but the yarn then rose to the following flight of fancy: These empty tins were to be filled with dry cement and loaded on camels, which were to be marched of us have called it a political bogey and some a world-menace, but these are extremist views—it is really the practical protest of Moslems against the exploitation of their spiritual and material resources by outsiders.

Pan-Islam (as its name implies) is a movement to weld together Moslems throughout the world regardless of nationality. The ethics and ideals of Islam are more attainable to ordinary human beings than those of Christianity: whether it is better to aim high and score a partial success or aim lower and achieve is a matter of personal opinion and need not be discussed here, but one tangible fact stands out—that Islam, with its easier moral standard and frequent physical discipline of attitudes and observances connected with obligatory prayer, enters far more into the daily life of its adherents than Christianity does with us. Hence pan-Islam is more than a spiritual movement: it is a practical, working proposition which has to be reckoned with when dealing with Moslems even in secular matters.

Pan-Islam is no new thing—it is as old as the Hejira, and then helped to knit together Moslem Arabs against their pagan compatriots who were persecuting them. In the palmy days of the Abbaside Caliphate it was quiescent enough, and men of all creeds were welcomed at Baghdad without water for days until they reached the Canal, when the pangs of thirst would compel them to rush madly into the water. The cement would solidify and the Faithful would march across on a composite bridge of camel and concrete. Our flotilla was to be penned in by similar means.

There must be something about a Turk that hypnotises an Egyptian. His country has suffered appallingly under Ottoman rule, and a pure-blooded Turk can seldom be decently civil to him and considers him almost beneath contempt. This is the conquering Tartar pose that has earned the Turk such detestation and final ruin in Arabia, but it seems to have fascinated the Egyptian like a rabbit in the presence of a python. Quite early in the Turkish invasion of Sinai a detachment of Egyptian camelry, operating in conjunction with the Bikanirs, deserted *en masse* to the enemy. It was at first supposed that they had been captured, but we afterwards heard of their being fêted somewhere in Palestine. On the other hand, an Egyptian battery did yeoman service on the Canal; I saw a pontoon that looked like a carelessly opened sardine-tin as a result of its attentions.

The most tragic aspect of this spurious and mischievous propaganda was its victims from

Indian regiments. The Indian Moslem as a rule has no illusions about the Turks, and will fight them at sight, but there will always be a few misguided bigots to whom a specious and dogmatic argument will appeal. There is no occasion to dwell on these cases, which were sporadic only and generally soon met with the fate incurred by attempted desertion to the enemy.

We looked on the movement as an insidious and dangerous disease and did our best to trace it to its source and stop the distributing channels. After events on the Canal had simmered down, I was seconded to Cairo to help tackle the movement there: to show how little hold it had over the minds of thinking Moslems I may mention that my colleague was a Pathan major who was a very strict Moslem and a first-rate fellow to boot.

We both served under an Anglo-Indian major belonging to the C.I.D., one of the most active little men I have ever met. There were also several "ferrets," or Intelligence agents, who came into close contact with the "suspects" and could be trusted up to a certain point if you looked sharply after them. This is as much as can be said for any of these men, though some are better, and some worse, than others.

On the Canal we employed numbers of them to keep us informed of the enemy's movements and used to check them with the aerial reconnaissance—they needed it. It did not take us long to find out that these sophisticated Sinaites had established an Intelligence bureau of their own. They used to meet their "opposite numbers" employed by the enemy at prearranged spots between the lines and swop information, thereby avoiding unnecessary toil or risk (the Sinaitic Bedouin loathes both) and obtaining news of interest for both sides. It was a magnificently simple scheme; its sole flaw was in failing to realise that some of us had played the Great Game before. We used to time our emissaries to their return and cross-check them where their wanderings intersected those of others—all were supposed to be trackers and one or two knew something about it. Of course they were searched and researched on crossing and returning to our outpost line, for they could not be trusted to refuse messages to or from the Turks. It was among this coterie that the brilliant idea originated of shaving a messenger's head, writing a despatch on his scalp, and then letting his hair grow before he started to deliver it. I doubt if any of our folk were thorough enough for this, but we tested for it occasionally, and an unpleasant job it was. Generally they would incur suspicion by their too speedy return and the nonchalant way in which they imparted tidings which would have driven them into ecstasies of self-appreciation had they obtained such by legitimate methods. Then a purposely false bit of information calculated to cause certain definite action on the other side would usually betray them. Some purists suggested a firing party as a fitting end for these gambits, but that would have been a waste. Such men have their uses, until they know they are suspected, as valuable channels of misinformation. No doubt the enemy knew this too, and that is how an Intelligence Officer earns his pay, by sifting grain from chaff as it comes in and sending out empty husks and mouldy news.

But to return to Cairo. We netted a good deal of small fry, but only landed one big fish during the time I was attached. He was a Mesopotamian and a very respectable old gentleman, who followed the calling of astrologer and peripatetic quack—a common combination and admirably adapted for distributing propaganda. He came from Stamboul through Athens with exemplary credentials, and might have got through to India, which was the landfall he proposed to make, if his propagandist energy had not led him to deviate on a small side-tour in Egypt. Here we got on his track, and I boarded the Port Said express at short notice while he and the "ferret" who had picked him up got into a third-class compartment lower down. As the agent made no signal after the train had pulled out, I knew our man had not got the bulk of his propaganda with him, otherwise I had powers to hold up the express, for it was more important to get his stuff than the man himself. At Port Said he had a chance of seeing me, thanks to the agent's clumsiness, and I had to shave my beard off and buy a sun-helmet in consequence, for I was travelling in the same ship along the Canal to see that he did not communicate with troops on either side of the bank, and on the slightest suspicion he would have put his stuff over the side. All went smoothly and he was arrested in Suez roads by plain-clothes men with a sackful of seditious literature for printing broadcast in India. Of course they arrested the "ferret" too, as is usual in these cases. I went ashore with them in the police-launch as a casual traveller and was amused to hear the agent rating the old man for not having prophesied this mishap when telling his fortune the night before.

The propagandist was merely interned in a place of security—it was not our policy to make martyrs of such men, especially when they were *bona fide* Ottoman subjects.

I was rather out of touch with the pan-Islamic movement during the summer of 1915, as my lungs had become seriously affected on the Canal, and the trouble became so acute that I had to spend two or three months in the hills of Cyprus. Before I had been there a week the G.O.C. troops in Egypt cabled for me to return and proceed to Aden as political officer with troops.

I was too ill then to move and had to cable to that effect. My chagrin at missing a "show" was much alleviated when I heard what the show was. As it had a marked effect on the pan-Islamic campaign by enhancing Turkish prestige, it is not out of place to give some account of it here.

While I was still on the Canal in February (1915) a "memo" was sent for my information from Headquarters at Cairo to say that the Turks had invaded the Aden protectorate at Dhala, where I once served on a boundary commission.

I noted the fact and presumed that Aden was quite able to cope with the situation, as the Turks had a most difficult terrain to traverse before they could get clear of the hills and reach the littoral, while the hinterland tribes are noted for their combatant instincts and efficiency in guerilla warfare, besides being anti-Turk. I had, however, in spite of many years' experience, failed to reckon with Aden apathy. True to the policy of *laissez faire* which was inaugurated when our Boundary Commission withdrew some twelve years ago, Aden had been depending for news of her own protectorate on office files and native report, especially on that much overrated friend and ally the Lahej sultanate. The Turks knew all about this, for the leakage of Aden affairs which trickles through Lahej and over the Yamen border is, and has been for years, a flagrant scandal.

The invasion at Dhala was a feint just to test the soundness of official slumber at Aden; the obvious route for a large force was down the Tiban valley, owing to the easier going and the permanent water-supply.

Our border-sultan (the Haushabi) was suborned with leisurely thoroughness all unknown to his next-door neighbour, that purblind sultanate at Lahej, unless the latter refrained from breaking Aden's holy calm with such unpleasant news.

In May Aden stirred in her sleep and sent out the Aden troop to reconnoitre. This fine body of Indian cavalry and camelry reported that affairs seemed serious up the Tiban valley; then inertia reasserted itself and they were recalled. Also the Lahej sultanate, in a spasm of economy, started disbanding the Arab levies collected for the emergency from the tribes of the remoter hinterland which have supplied fine mercenaries to many oriental sultanates for many centuries.

The watchful Turk, with his unmolested spy system, had noted every move of these pitiful blunders, and, at the psychological moment, came pouring down the Tiban valley some 3,000 strong with another 5,000 Arab levies. They picked up the Haushabi on the way, whose main idea was to get a free kick at Lahej, just as an ordinary human boy will serve some sneak and prig to whom a slack schoolmaster has relegated his own obvious duty of supervision. To do that inadequate sultanate justice, it tried to bar the way with its own trencher-fed troops and such levies as it had, but was brushed aside contemptuously by the hardier levies opposed to it and the overwhelming fire of the Turkish field batteries. Then a distraught and frantic palace emitted mounted messengers to Aden for assistance like minute-guns from a sinking ship.

Aden behaved exactly like a startled hen. She ran about clucking and collecting motor-cars, camel transport, anything. The authorities dared not leave their pet sultan in the lurch—questions might be asked in the House. On the other hand they had made no adequate arrangements to protect him. Just as a demented hen will leave her brood at the mercy of a hovering kite to round up one stray chick instead of sitting tight and calling it in under her wing, so Aden made a belated and insane attempt to save Lahej.

The Aden Movable Column, a weak brigade of Indians, young Territorials, and guns, marched out at 2 p.m. on July 4, *i.e.* at the hottest time of day, in the hottest season of the year and the hottest part of the world. Motor-cars were used to convey the infantry of the advanced guard, but the main body had to march in full equipment with ammunition. The casualties from sunstroke were appalling. The late G.O.C. troops in Egypt mentioned them to me in hundreds, and one of the Aden "politicals" told me that not a dozen of the territorial battalion remained effective at the end of the day. Many were bowled over by the heat before they had gone two miles.

Most of the native camel transport, carrying water, ammunition and supplies,—and yet unescorted and not even attended by a responsible officer—sauntered off into the desert and vanished from the ken of that ill-fated column.

Meanwhile the advanced guard of 250 men (mostly Indians) and two 10-pounder mountain-guns pushed on with all speed to Lahej, which was being attacked by several thousand Turks and Turco-Arabs with 15-pounder field batteries and machine-guns. They found the palace and part of the town on fire when they arrived, and fought the Turks hand-to-hand in the streets. They held on all through that sweltering night, and only retired when dawn showed them the hopeless nature of their task and the fact that they were being outflanked. They fell back on the main body, which had stuck halfway at a wayside well (Bir Nasir) marked so obviously by ruins that even Aden guides could not miss it. Shortage of water was the natural result of sitting over a well that does not even supply a settlement, but merely the ordinary needs of wayfarers.

This well is marked on the Aden protectorate survey map (which is procurable by the general public) as Bir Muhammad, its full name being Bir Muhammad Nasir. There are five wells supplying settlements within half an hour's walk of it on either side of the track, but when we remember that the column's field-guns got no further owing to heavy sand, and that the aforesaid track is frequently traversed by ordinary *tikkagharries*, we realise the local knowledge available.

The column straggled back to the frontier town of Sheikh Othman, which they prepared to defend, but Simla, by this time thoroughly alarmed, ordered them back for the defence of Aden, and they returned without definite achievement other than the accidental shooting of the Lahej sultan. This was hardly the fault of the heroic little band which reached Lahej; that ill-starred potentate was escaping with his mounted retinue before dawn and cantered on top of an Indian outpost without the formality of answering their challenge. He was brought away in a motor-car and died at Aden a few days later—another victim to this deplorable blunder. Any intelligent and timely grasp of the enemy's strength and intention would have given the poor man ample time to pack his inlaid hookahs, Persian carpets, and other palace treasures and withdraw in safety to Aden while our troops made good the Sheikh Othman line along the British frontier. I am presuming that Aden was too much taken by surprise to have met the Turks in a position of her own choosing while they were still entangled in hilly country where levies of the right sort could have harried them to some purpose, backed by disciplined, unspent troops and adequate guns. What I wish to impress is that the Intelligence Department at Aden must have been abominably served and organised, for I decline to believe that *any* G.O.C. would have attempted such an enterprise with such a force and at such a time had he any information as to the real nature of his task. As it was, the British town of Sheikh Othman, within easy sight of Aden across the harbour, was held by the Turks until a reinforcing column came down from the Canal and drove them out of it, while the protectorate has been overrun by the Turks and the Turco-Arabs until long after the armistice, and the state of British prestige there can be imagined.

Official attempts to gloze over the incident would have been amusing if they were not pathetic. Needless to say they did not deceive Moslems in Egypt or the rest of Arabia.

Here is the most accurate account they gave the public:

"TURKS AND ADEN.

"ENGAGEMENT AT LAHEJ.

"The India Office issued the following *communiqué* last night through the Press Bureau:

"'In consequence of rumours that a Turkish force from the Yamen had crossed the frontier of the Aden Hinterland and was advancing towards Lahej, the General Officer Commanding at Aden recently dispatched the Aden Camel Troop to reconnoitre.

"'They reported the presence of a Turkish force with field-guns and a large number of Arabs and fell back on Lahej, where they were reinforced by the advance guard of the Aden Movable Column consisting of 250 rifles and two 10-pounder guns.

"'Our force at Lahej was attacked by the enemy on July 4 by a force of several thousand Turks with twenty guns and large numbers of Arabs, and maintained its position in face of the enemy artillery's fire until night, when part of Lahej was in flames. During the night some hand-to-hand fighting took place, and the enemy also commenced to outflank us.

"'Meanwhile the remainder of the Aden Movable Column was marching towards Lahej, but was delayed by water difficulties and heavy going. It was therefore decided that the small force at Lahej should fall back.

"'The retirement was carried out successfully in the early morning of July 5, and the detachment joined the rest of the column at Bir Nasir. Our troops, however, were suffering considerably from the great heat and the shortage of water, and their difficulties were increased by the desertion of Arab transport followers. It was therefore decided to fall back to Aden, and this was done without the enemy attempting to follow up.

"'Our losses included three British officers wounded: names will be communicated later. We took one Turkish officer (a major) and thirteen men prisoners.'"

Aden seems to have made no attempt to stem the tide of Turkish influence while she could. The best fighting tribe in the protectorate stretches along the coast and far inland north-east of Aden, and its capital is only a few hours' steam from that harbour. The Turks made every effort to win over this important tribal unit, which might have been a grave menace on their left flank. Its sultan made frequent representations to Aden for even a gunboat to show itself off his port, but to no purpose. After the Turks had succeeded in alienating those of his tribe they could get at, or who could get at them, a tardy political visit was paid by sea from Aden. The indignant old sultan came aboard and spoke his mind. "You throw your friends on the midden," he said bitterly, and departed to establish a *modus vivendi* on his own account with the Turks.

The situation at Aden has had a marked effect in bolstering up the Turkish campaign of spurious pan-Islamism, and those of us who have been dealing with chiefs in other parts of Arabia have met it at every turn. It is idle to blame individuals—the whole system is at fault. The policy of non-interference which the Liberal Government introduced, after the Boundary Commission had finished its task and withdrawn, has been overstrained by the Aden authorities to such an extent that they would neither keep in direct personal touch themselves nor let anyone else do so.

As an explorer and naturalist whose chief work has lain for years in that country, I have made every effort to continue my researches there until my persistency has incurred official persecution. The serious aspect of this attitude is that at a time when accurate and up-to-date knowledge of the hinterland would have been invaluable it was not available. The pernicious policy of selecting any one chief (unchecked by a European) to keep her posted as to affairs in her own protectorate has been followed blindly by

Aden to disaster. The excuse in official circles there is that the Haushabi sultan had been suborned by the Turks without their knowledge and he had prevented any information from getting through Lahej to them. Can there be any more damning indictment of such a system?

The Aden incident is similar to the Mesopotamian medical muddle, both being due to sporadic dry-rot in high places which the test of war revealed. The loyalty of its princes and the devotion of its army prove that there is nothing fundamentally wrong with British rule in India to command such sentiments, but some of those mandarins who have had wide control of human affairs and destinies have ignored a situation until it was forcibly thrust upon them and have fumbled with it disastrously. It is difficult to bring such people to book, for they shuffle responsibility from one to the other or take refuge in the truly oriental pose of heaven-born officialdom. Such types should be obsolete even in India by now, but this war has proved that they are not, and when their inanities fritter away gallant lives and trail British prestige in the dust they need rebuke. I hope some day, if I live, to deal faithfully with Aden's hinterland policy.

In the autumn of 1915 I was fit enough to join the Red Sea maritime patrol as political officer with the naval rank of lieutenant. Our duties were to harry the Turk without hurting the Arab, to blockade the Arabian coast against the Turk while allowing dhow-traffic with foodstuffs consigned to Arab merchants and steamer-cargoes of food for the alleged use of pilgrims to go through. Incidentally we had to keep the eastern highway free of mines and transportable submarines, prevent the passage of spies between Arabia and Egypt, and fetch and carry as the shore-folk required.

Taking it all round, it was not an easy job, but I think the blockade presented the most complex features. You knew where you were with spies—anyone with the necessary experience could spot a doubtful customer as soon as the dhow that carried him came alongside; and irregular but frequent visits at the various ports soon put a stop to the mine-industry and prevented any materialisation of the submarine menace except in reports from Aden which caused me a good many additional trips in an armed steam-cutter to "go, look, see."

But the problems presented by the blockade required some solving with very little time for the operation, and if your solution was not approved by the authorities on the beach they lost no time in letting you know it—usually by wireless, which was picked up by most ships in the patrol by the time it reached you.

The basic idea was that if in doubt it was better to let stuff through to the Turks than pinch Hejazi bellies and get ourselves disliked. In theory this was perfectly sound, for we wanted the Hejaz to like us well enough to fight on our side, and only the Huns think you can get people to love you by afflicting them. In practice, however, we soon found that the Hejazi merchants were selling direct to the Turks and letting their fellow-countrymen have what was left at the highest possible price. On top of it all India started a howl that her pilgrims in the Hejaz were starving, and we had to defer to this outcry. I have never had to legislate for highly-civilised Moslems with a taste for agitation, but I have always sympathised with those who have, and could quite appreciate India's position in the matter. Still, after comparing her relief cargoes with the number of her pilgrims in the country and finding that each had enough to feed him for the rest of his natural life, I ventured to ask that this wholesale charity might cease, more especially as these big steamer-cargoes were dealt with much as the dhow-borne cereals and chiefly benefited the Turks and local profiteers.

As regards dhows, our rule was to allow coastal

traffic from Jeddah and empties returning there, as it tended to distribute food among the Arabs and get it away from the Turks. Dhows bringing cargo from the African coast or from Aden were permitted, provided they did not carry contraband of war; this permitted native cereals, such as millet, but barred wheat and particularly barred barley, which the local Arab does not eat for choice, but which the Turks wanted very badly for their cavalry.

In this connection a typical incident may be mentioned as illustrating the sort of thing we were up against.

The ship I was serving in at the time lay off Jeddah and had three boats down picketing the dhow-channels leading in to that reef-girt harbour, for which dhows were making like homing bees. In such cases my post was usually on the bridge, while the ship's interpreter and Arab-speaking Seedee-boys went away in the boats. The dhows were reached and their papers examined, then allowed to proceed if all was in order. Otherwise the officer examining signalled the facts and awaited instructions. Usually it was some technical point which I could waive, but on this occasion one of the cutters made a signal to the effect that barley in bulk had been found in one dhow. I was puzzled, because all the dhows were from Suakin or further south, quite outside the barley-belt, except on very high ground which rarely exports cereals. However, the signal was repeated, and I had to have the dhow alongside. Meanwhile the "owner" was anxious to get steerage-way, for we were not at anchor and in very ticklish soundings; so I slid off the bridge and had a sample of the grain handed up to me: it was a species of millet, looking very like pearl-barley as "milled" for culinary purposes. I shouted to the *reis* to go where he liked as long as he kept clear of our propellers, which thereupon gave a ponderous flap or two as if to emphasise my remarks, and he bore away from us rejoicing. In the ward-room later on I rallied that cutter's officer on his error. "Well, it was just like the barley one sees in soup," was his defence.

In the southern part of the Red Sea, which was handled politically from Aden, the problems of blockade were even more complex, for there even arms and ammunition were allowed between certain ports to meet the convenience of the Idrisi chief, who was theoretically at war with the Turks, but rather diffident about putting his principles into practice, especially after the Turkish success outside Aden.

This meant that the sorely-tried officers responsible for the conduct of the blockade in those waters had crabbed from decide on a cargo of illicit-looking rifles and cartridges, not of Government make, but purchased from private firms and guaranteed by a filthy scrap of paper inscribed with crabbed Arabic which carried no conviction. All they had to help them was the half-educated ship's interpreter, with no knowledge of the political situation, for Aden had not an officer available for this work. To enhance the difficulties of the position, some of these coastal chiefs were importing contraband of war to sell to the Turks for private gain. Up north there were no difficulties with illicit arms; we allowed a reasonable number per dhow, provided that they were the private property of the crew, and when rifles were dished out to our Arab friends the Navy delivered the goods, which were all of Government mark and pattern.

The political aspect of the blockade required delicate handling anywhere along the Arabian littoral of the Red Sea, but especially so on the Hejazi coast. We were at war with the Turks but not with the Arabs, whom it was our business to approach as friends if they would let us. The Turks, however, used Arab levies freely against us whose truculence was much increased on finding they could make hostile demonstrations with impunity, as the patrol only fired on the Turkish uniform, since few people can distinguish between a Turco-Arab gendarme and an armed tribesman at long range unless they know both breeds intimately.

The general standard of honour and good faith at most places along the Arabian littoral is not high, even from an Oriental point of view, and is nowhere lower than on the Hejazi coast. Frequently an unattached tribesman would take a shot at a reconnoitring cutter on general principles and then rush off to the nearest Turkish post with the information and a demand for bakshish, and there were several attempts (one successful) to lure a landing party on to a well-manned but carefully hidden position. As for the actual levies, they would solemnly man prepared positions within easy range of even a 3-pounder when we visited their tinpot ports, relying on us not to fire, and telling their compatriots what they would do if we did.

Even when examining dhows one had to be on one's guard, and it was best not to board them to leeward and so run the risk of having their big, bellying mainsail let go on top of you and getting scuppered while entangled in its folds. African dhows could generally be trusted not to resist search, for when a *reis* has got his owners or agents at a civilised port like Suakin he likes to keep respectable even if he *is* smuggling. Our chief difficulty with such craft, before we tightened the blockade, was due to the nonchalant manner in which they put to sea and behaved when at sea. Their skippers had the sketchiest idea of what constituted proper clearance papers and why such papers must agree with their present voyage. Their confidence too in our integrity, though touching, was often embarrassing. One of our rules was that considerable sums in gold must be given up against a signed voucher realisable at Port Sudan. I was never very brisk at counting large sums of money, and one day when hove to off Jeddah there were five dhows rubbing their noses alongside, with about £800 in gold between them and very little time to deal with them, as we were in shoal water with no way on the ship. My operations were not facilitated by the biggest Crœsus of the lot producing some £400 in five different currencies from various parts of his apparel and stating that he had no idea how much there was but would abide by my decision. I believe he expected me to give him a receipt in round hundreds and take the "oddment," as we call it in Warwickshire, for myself. As it was, I was down half a sovereign or so over the transaction, having given him the benefit of the doubt over two measly little gold coins of unascertainable value.

Some of them were just as happy-go-lucky in their seamanship, though skilful enough in handling their outlandish craft. Early one morning, about fifty miles out of Jeddah, I boarded a becalmed dhow and found them with the dregs of one empty water-skin between a dozen men. Not content with putting to sea with a single *mussick* of water, they had hove to and slept all night, and so dropped the night breeze, which would have carried them to Jeddah before it died down. We gave them water and their position, but I told the *reis* that he was putting more strain on the mercy of Allah than he was, individually, entitled to

But the craft that plied along the Hejazi coast were sinister customers and wanted watching. Some time before I joined the patrol one of our ships was lying a long way out off Um-Lejj, as the water is shallow, and her duty-boat was working close in-shore examining coastal craft. One of these had some irregularity about her and was sent out to the ship with a marine and a bluejacket in charge while the cutter continued her task. That dhow stood out to sea as if making for the ship and then proceeded along the coast. The cutter, still busied with other dhows, presumed that the first craft had reported alongside the ship and been allowed to proceed; the ship naturally regarded her as a craft that had been examined and permitted to continue her journey. And that is all we ever knew for certain of her or the fate of our two men. Their previous record puts desertion out of the question; besides, no sane men would desert to a barren, inhospitable coast among semi-hostile fanatics whose language was unknown to them. On the other hand, the men were, of course, fully armed, and there were but five of the dhow's crew all told, of whom two were not able-bodied. There must have been the blackest treachery—probably the unfortunate men goodnaturedly helped with the running gear and were knocked on the head while so engaged. Their bodies would, no doubt, have been put over the side when the dhow was out of sight, and their rifles sold inland at a fancy price.

When I first joined the patrol we were not allowed to bombard or land at any point between the mouth of the Gulf of Akaba and the Hejaz southern border. The Turkish fort up at Akaba had been knocked about a good deal by various ships of the patrol, and the whole place was uninhabited; but we visited it frequently, as drifting mines were put in up there, having been taken off the rail at Maan and brought down to the head of the gulf, in section, by camel. I always suspected the existence of a Turkish observation-post, but no signs of occupation had been seen for a long time till H.M.S. "Fox" went up one dark night without a light showing. All dead-lights were shipped, and dark blue electric bulbs replaced the usual ones where a light of some sort was essential and visible from out-board. The padre, who had opened the "vicarage" dead-light about an inch to get a breath of air, was promptly spotted by an indignant Number One who said that it made the ship look like a floating gin palace. This must have been a pardonable hyperbole, for the signal-fires ashore which used to herald our approach from afar were not lit.

We were off Akaba at peep of day, and two armed cutters raced each other to the beach. I went with the one that made for the stone jetty in the middle front of the town; we had to jump out into four feet of water, as the port has deteriorated a good deal since Solomon used it and called it Eziongeber. A careful search revealed no one in the town, but water had been drawn recently from the well inside the fort, and a mud hut out in the desert behind the town seemed a likely covert to draw.

The cutter's officer accompanied me, leaving the crew ensconced in the cemetery, which was a wise move, for, when we were close to the hut, heavy fire was opened on us from a hidden trench some three hundred yards away. We both dropped and rolled into a shallow depression caused by rain-wash, where we lay as flat as we could while the flat-nosed soft lead bullets kicked sand and shingle down the backs of our necks. As we had only revolvers—expecting resistance, if any, to be made among the houses—we could not reply, but the ship handed out a few rounds of percussion shrapnel which shook the Turks up enough for us to withdraw. Fortunately for us, they were using black powder, and outside four hundred yards one has time to avoid the bullet by dropping instantly at the smoke. Otherwise they should have bagged us in spite of the support of our covering party in the cemetery, for the ground was quite open and so dusty that they could see the break of their heavy picket-bullets to a nicety.

We landed in force an hour later and turned them out of it. On returning, the men who searched the hut (which the ship's guns had knocked endways) brought me a budget of correspondence. It was chiefly addressed to the officer in charge and told me that the detachment was Syrian, which I had already suspected from their using the early pattern Mauser. It gave other useful information, and the men did well to bring it along; but I would have given much to have found some channel through which I could return it. Most of it was private; there were several congratulatory cards crudely illuminated in colours by hand for the feast of Muled-en-Nebi (the birthday of the Prophet), which corresponds with our Christmas. There was also a letter from the officer's wife enclosing a half-sheet of paper on which a baby hand had imprinted a smeared outline in ink. It bore the inscription "From your son Ahmed—his hand and greeting."

Early in the spring of 1916 we managed to persuade the political folk at Cairo to extend our sphere of action. I had particularly marked down Um-Lejj as containing a well-manned Turkish fort which could be knocked about without damaging other buildings in the town if we were careful. It was also a rallying-point for Turkish influence, and it was not conducive to our prestige or politically desirable that it should flourish unmolested.

I was in the "Fox" again for that occasion, she being the senior ship of the patrol and the only one that could land an adequate force if required.

The evening before we anchored far out on the fishing-grounds of Hasani Island, and I managed to pick up a fisherman who knew where the Turkish hidden position was, outside the town, and, having been held a prisoner once in their Customs building, could point that out too. Next morning we stood slowly in for Um-Lejj with the steam-cutter groping ahead for the channel, which is about as tortuous a piece of navigation as you can get off this coast, and that is saying a good deal.

When we cleared for action I went to my usual post on the bridge with the S.N.O. and took my fisherman-friend with me. The civil population was streaming out of the town across the open plain in all directions like ants from an overturned ant-hill, probably realising that we meant business this time. This was all to the good, as otherwise I should have had to go close in with the steam-cutter, a white flag and a megaphone to warn Arab civilians; thus giving the Turks time to clear, besides the chance of a sitting-shot at us if they thought my address to the townsfolk a violation of the rules of war, which, technically, it might be.

However, the fort was a fixture and our business

was first of all with it. Standing close in, the ship turned southwards and moved slowly abreast of the town. The port battery of four-point-sevens loaded with H.E. and the two six-inchers fore and aft swung out-board and followed suit. The occasion called for fine shooting, as a minaret rose just to the right of the fort, and the houses were so massed about it that there was only one clear shot—up the street leading from the beach past the main gate.

"At the southern gate of the fort, each gun to fire as it comes to bear up the street from the water-side."

As I turned my glasses on the big portico of the southern gate, out stepped a Turkish officer who regarded us intently; the next instant the bridge shook to the crashing concussion of our forward six-inch, and through a drifting haze of gas-fume I saw him blotted out by the orange flash of lyddite and an up-flung pall of dust and *débris*.

There was a pause, cut short by the clap of the bursting shell reverberating like thunder against the foot-hills beyond the town.

A little naked boy ran in an attitude of terrified dismay up the water-street just as the first four-point-seven fired. I saw him through my glasses duck his head between his arms, then dive panic-stricken through a doorway as the fort was smitten again in dust and thunder. "Was the poor little beggar hit?"

"No, sir, only scared."

While the target was still veiled in its dust the second four-point-seven spoke, and the minaret disappeared from view behind a dun-coloured shroud.

"Cease fire" sounded at once. "Who fired that gun? Take him off," came in tones of stern rebuke from the bridge. Luckily the minaret showed intact as the dust drifted clear and firing continued.

As the fort crumbled under our guns, Turkish soldiers began to break cover at various points of the town and fled across the plain. The cutter, in-shore, opened with Maxim-fire, and so accurately that we could see the sombre-clad figures lying here and there or seeking frantically for cover, while an Arab in their vicinity, leading a leisurely camel, continued his stroll inland unperturbed. We drove the main body out of their hidden position and into the hills with well-timed shrapnel, and finished up by demolishing the Customs (where a lot of ammunition blew up), to the temporary satisfaction of my fisherman, who was curled up in a çorner of the bridge, nearly stunned by the shock of modern ordnance in spite of the cotton-wool I had made him put in his ears. Before we picked up our cutter the civil population was already streaming back.

The incident is worth noting in view of remarks made by a popular fiction-monger in one of his latest works, that indiscriminate aerial raids on civil centres in England are on the same level of humanity as naval bombardments.

I visited the fishing-banks off Hasani Island a week or so after to get the latest news of Um-Lejj, which came from Turkish sources. There was one civilian casualty—a woman who was in the Turkish concealed position. No casualties among Turkish officers, but one of them left in charge of the fort had disappeared. There were bits of the fort left, but the Commandant had moved his headquarters to the school-house within the precincts of the mosque—sagacious soul. The object-lesson which we gave the Arabs at Um-Lejj put a check to their irresponsible sniping of boats and landing-parties, though one could always expect a little trouble with an Arab dhow running contraband for the Turks. In these cases their guilty consciences usually gave them away. Returning to the coast toward Jeddah unexpectedly, having played the well-worn ruse of "the cat's away," we sighted a small dhow close in-shore, and should have left her alone as she was in shoal-water, but, on standing in to get a nearer view of her, she headed promptly for the beach and ran aground, disgorging more men than such a craft should carry.

I went away in the duty cutter to investigate, and we had barely realised that she was heavily loaded with kerosene in tins (a heinous contraband) when the fact was emphasised by a sputtering rifle-fire from the scrub along the beach. The ship very soon put a stop to that demonstration with a round or two of shrapnel, while we busied ourselves with the dhow. There was no hope of salving her, as she had almost ripped the keel off her when she took the ground and sat on the bottom like a dilapidated basket. We broached enough tins to start a conflagration, lit a fuse made of a strip of old turban soaked in kerosene, and backed hard from her vicinity, for the kerosene was low-flash common stuff as marked on the cases, and to play at snapdragon in half an acre of blazing oil is an uninviting pastime. However, she just flared without exploding, and we continued our cruise up the coast just in time to overhaul at racing speed a perfect regatta of dhows heeling over to every stitch of canvas in their efforts to make Jeddah before we could get at them, for they had seen the smoke of that burning oil-dhow and realised that the cat was about. Good money is paid at Cowes to see no more spirited sailing—we had to put a shot across the bows of the leading dhow before they would abandon the race.

There was always trouble off Jeddah—the approaches to that reef-girt harbour lend themselves to blockade-running dhows with sound local knowledge on board. At night, especially, they had an advantage and would play "Puss-in-the-Corner" until the cutter lost patience, and a flickering pin-point of light stabbed the velvet black of the middle watch, asking permission to fire; one rifle-shot fired high would stop the game, and I made them come alongside and take a wigging for annoying the cutter and turning me out; there was seldom anything wrong about the dhow—it was sheer cussedness.

All through the early part of 1916 we were keeping in touch with the Sharif of Mecca by means of envoys, whom we landed where they listed, away from the Turks, picking them up at times and places indicated by them. Sharif Husein had long chafed under Turkish suzerainty, in spite of his subsidy and the deference which policy compelled them to accord him. He knew that the Hejaz could never realise its legitimate aspirations under Ottoman rule, which was a blight on all Arab progress and prosperity, as the

Young Turkish party was hardly Moslem at heart, being more national (that is Tartar)—certainly not pro-Arab.

Husein's difficulty was to get his own people to rise together and throw off the Turkish yoke, for the Hejazi tribesman, especially between the coast and Mecca, has long been more of a brigand than a warrior, as any pilgrim will tell you. Such folk are apt to jib at hammer-and-tongs fighting, and of course we could not land troops to assist them, as it would have violated the sacred soil that cradled Islam and merely stiffened the bogus *jihad* which the Turks had proclaimed against us, besides compromising the Sharif with his own tribesmen.

The Hejazis' ingenuous idea was to go on taking money from us, the Turks and the Sharif, while—thanks to our lenient blockade—a regular dhow-traffic fed them. We did not approve of this Utopian policy, and the fall of Kut brought matters to a climax. After certain communications had passed between the representatives of His Majesty's Government and the Sharif, it was decided to tighten the blockade and so induce the gentle Hejazi to declare himself. The day was fixed, May, 15, on and after which date no traffic whatever was to be permitted with the Arabian coast other than that specially sanctioned by Government. In palaver thereon I managed to get local fishing-craft exempted. The fisher-folk are not combatants either on empty stomachs or full ones, and could be relied on to consume their own fish in that climate unless very close to a market, where the pinch would be great enough to make them exchange it for foodstuffs, thus helping the situation we wished to bring about. I knew that all *bona fide* fishing-craft were easily recognisable by their rig and comparatively small size, and hoped that good will would combine with freedom of movement to make these folk useful agents for Intelligence.

I heard with some relief that the movements of the patrol would place H.M.S. "Hardinge" (a roomy ship of the Indian Marine) on station duty off Jeddah, which was to be my post while the enhanced blockade was in force—there are few more trying seasons than early summer in those waters. I joined her from Suez the day after the blockade was closed, and found her keeping guard over a perfect fleet of dhows. There were about three dozen craft with over three hundred people on board, for many native passengers were trying to make Jeddah before we shut down. The feckless mariners in charge had made the usual oriental calculation that a day more or less did not matter, but found to their horror that the Navy was more precise on these points—and there they were.

The first thing to ensure was that the crew, and especially the passengers, among whom were a good many women and children, did not suffer from privation. This had already been ably seen to by the ship's officers—I merely went round the fleet to sift any genuine complaints from the discontent natural to the situation in which their own slackness had placed them. I insisted on hearing only one complaint at a time, otherwise it would have been pandemonium afloat, for they were anchored close enough together to converse with each other; vociferous excuses for their unpunctuality were brushed aside, legitimate requests for more water or food or condensed milk for the children or more adequate shelter for the women from the sun were attended to at once, and our floating village quieted down.

The craft were all much the same type of small dhow or *sanbuk* which frequents the Red Sea and the Gulf of Aden, having little in common with the big-bellied buggalows which ply with rice and dates between the Persian Gulf and Indian ports but do not come into the Red Sea. These were much smaller and saucier-looking craft, some fifty to eighty feet long, with a turn of speed and raking masts. All were lugger-rigged with lateen sails, and only the poop and bows were decked, the bulwarks being heightened with strips of matting to prevent seas from breaking in-board. Sanitary arrangements were provided for by a box-like cubby-hole overhanging the boat's side; inexperienced officers often take it for a vantage-point to heave the lead from, and only find out too late after attempting to board there, that things are not always what they seem.

These little vessels are practically the corsair type of Saracenic sailing-galley which used to infest the Barbary coast in days gone by. They do everything different from our occidental methods. For example, they reef and furl their tall lateens from the peak, and have to send a man up the long tapering gaff to do it. Their masts rake forward and not aft, which enables them to swing gaff, sail, and sheet round in front of the mast when they come about, instead of keeping the sheet aft and dipping the butt of the gaff with the sail to the other side of the mast, which would be an impossibility for that rig, as the butt of their enormous mainyard or gaff is bowsed permanently down in the bows, while the soaring peak may be nearly a hundred feet above the water. Cooking was done over charcoal in a kerosene tin half full of sand, and the "first-class" passengers lived under an improvised awning on the poop, the women's quarters being under that gimcrack structure. All the same, they are good sea-boats and remarkably fast, especially *on* a wind, quite unlike the big-decked buggalows which are built for cargo capacity and have real cabins aft but sail like a haystack on a barge.

It was inhuman (as well as an infernal nuisance) to keep all those people sweltering indefinitely at sea; on the other hand, our orders as to the strict maintenance of the blockade were explicit. The "owner" and I conferred and decided that the situation could be met by transferring their cargo to the ship and letting the dhows beach. This was referred and approved by wireless. The job took us some days, as the weather was rather unfavourable and all the cargoes had to be checked by manifest with a view to restitution later. Each dhow as she was cleared had to make for the shore and dismast or beach so that she could not steal out at night and add to the difficulties of the blockade. None attempted to evade this order, most carried out both alternatives; perhaps a casual reminder that they would be within observation and gunfire of the ship had some influence on their action.

Hitherto the Turco-Teutonic brand of Holy War had been fairly successful. The Allied thrust at the Dardanelles and Gallipoli had failed, the Aden Protectorate was in Turkish hands, we had spent a most unpleasant Easter in Sinai, and Kut had fallen. Still, the Turks were soon to realise that a wrongly-invoked *jihad*, like a mishandled musket, can recoil heavily, and, before the end of May, signs were not wanting that trouble was brewing for them in the Hejaz.

We were in close touch with the shore through fishing-canoes by day and secret emissaries by night, who brought us news that some German "officers" had been done to death by Hejazi tribesmen some eight hours' journey north of Jeddah. They had evidently been first overpowered and bound, then stabbed in the stomach with the huge two-handed dagger which the Hejazis use, and finally decapitated, as a Turkish rescue party which hurried to the spot found their headless and practically disembowelled corpses with their hands tied behind them. Their effects came through our hands in due course, and we ascertained that the party consisted of Lieut.-Commander von Moeller (late of a German gunboat interned at Tsing-Tao) and five reservists whom he had picked up in Java. They had landed on the South Arabian coast in March, had visited Sanaa, the capital of Yamen, and had come up the Arabian coast of the Red Sea by dhow, keeping well inside the Farsan bank, which is three hundred miles long and a serious obstacle to patrol work. They had landed at Konfida, north of the bank, and reached Jeddah by camel on May 5. Against the advice of the Turks they continued their journey by land, as they had no chance of eluding our northern patrol at sea. They were more than a year too late to emulate the gallant (and lucky) "Odyssey" of the Emden's landing-party from Cocos Islands up the Red Sea coast in the days when our blockade was more lenient and did not interfere with coasting craft. They hoped to reach Maan and so get on the rail for Stamboul and back to Germany, as the Sharif would not sanction their coming to the sacred city of Medina, which is the rail-head for the Damascus–Hejaz railway. After so staunch a journey they deserved a better fate. Among their kit was a tattered and blood-stained copy of my book on the Aden hinterland.*

Meanwhile affairs ashore were simmering to boiling-point, and on the night of June 9 we commenced a bombardment of carefully located Turkish positions, firing by "director"

* "The Land of Uz," Macmillan.

to co-operate with an Arab attack which was due then but did not materialise till early next morning, and was then but feebly delivered. We found out later that the rifles and ammunition we had delivered on the beach some distance south of Jeddah to the Sharif's agents in support of this attack had been partly diverted to Mecca and partly hung up by a squabble with their own camel-men for more cash.

We continued the bombardment on the night of the 11th and were in action most of the day on the 12th, shelling the Turkish positions north of Jeddah, which we had located by glass and the co-operation of friendly fishing-craft who gave us the direction by signal. During the morning the Hejazis made an abortive and aimless attack along the beach north of Jeddah, and so masked our own supporting fire, while the Turks gave them more than they wanted.

By this time the senior ship and others had joined us, and the S.N.O. approved of my landing with a party of Indian signallers to maintain closer touch with their operations, provided that Arab headquarters would guarantee our safety as regards their own people. This they were unable to do.

The bombardment grew more and more strenuous and searching as other ships joined in and our knowledge of the Turkish positions became more accurate. On the 15th it culminated with the arrival of a seaplane carrier and heavy bombing of the Ottoman trenches which our flat-trajectory naval guns could hardly reach. The white flag went up before sunset, and next day there were *pourparlers* which led to an unconditional surrender on June 17, 1916.

Mecca had fallen just before, and Taif surrendered soon after, leaving Medina as the only important town still held by the Turks in the Hejaz.

We began pouring food and munitions into Jeddah as soon as it changed hands; for the rest of this cruise my ship was a sort of parcels-delivery van, and when the parcel happens to be an Egyptian mountain battery its delivery is an undertaking.

My personal contact with the Turks and their ill-omened *jihad* ended soon after, as I was invalided from service afloat, but I kept in touch as an Intelligence-wallah on the beach and followed the rest of it with interest.

They got Holy War with a vengeance. The Sharif's sons (more especially the Emirs Feisal and Abdullah, who had been trained at the Stamboul Military Academy), ably assisted by zealous and skilled British officers as mine-planters and aerial bombers, harried outlying posts and the Hejaz railway line north of Medina incessantly.

The Turkish positions at Wejh fell to the Red Sea flotilla, reinforced by the flagship. I should like to have been there, if only to have seen the Admiral sail in to the proceedings with a revolver in his fist and the *élan* of a sub-lieutenant. The Hejazis failed to synchronise, as usual, so the Navy dispensed with their support.

On February 24, 1917, Kut was wrested from the Turks again; on March 11 they lost Baghdad; on November 7 their Beersheba-Gaza front was shattered, and Jerusalem fell on December 9.

Early next year Jericho was captured (February 21), a British column from Baghdad reached the Caspian in August, and after a final, victorious British offensive in Palestine the unholy alliance of Turkish pan-Islamism and German *Kultur* got its death-blow when Emir Feisal galloped into Damascus.

The Turks had drawn the blade of *jihad* from its pan-Islamic scabbard in vain; its German trade-mark was plainly stamped on it. There had been widespread organisation against us, and the serpent's eggs of sedition and revolt had been hatched in centres scattered all over the eastern hemisphere, but their venomous progeny had been crushed before they became formidable.

As a world-force this band of pan-Islamism had failed because it had been invoked by the wrong people for a wrong purpose. Such a movement should at least have as its driving power some great spiritual crisis: this Turco-German manifestation of it had its origin in self-interest, and if successful would have immolated Arabia on the demoniac altar of *Weltpolitik*. Seyid Muhammed er-Rashid Ridha, a descendant of the Prophet and one of the greatest Arab theologians living, has voiced the verdict of Islam on this unscrupulous and self-seeking adventure in a trenchant article published in September, 1916. He showed up Enver and his Unionist party as an atheist among atheists who had deprived the Sultan of his rightful power and Islam of its religious head, and contrasted their conduct with that of the British, who exempted the Hejaz from the blockade enforced against the rest of the Ottoman Empire until it became quite clear that the Turks were benefiting chiefly by that exemption, and who, out of respect for the holy places of Islam, refrained from making that country a theatre of war.

True to the Teutonic tradition, the movement had been laboriously organised, but lacked psychic insight, for the Turk is too much of a Tartar and too little of a Moslem to appreciate the Arab mind, and the German ignored it, rooting with eager, guttural grunts among the carefully cultivated religious prejudices of Islam like a hog hunting truffles until whacked out of it by the irate cultivators.

The following incident may serve to illustrate their crude tactics. Soon after the Turks came into the war the mullah of the principal mosque at Damascus was told to announce *jihad* against the British from his pulpit on the following Friday in accordance with an order from the Grand Mufti at Stamboul. The poor man appears to have jibbed considerably and sent his family over the Nejd border to be out of reach of Turkish persecution. Finally he decided to conform, but when he climbed the steps of his " minbar " and scanned his congregation he saw a group of German officers wearing tarbouches with a look of almost porcine complacency. His fear fell from him in a gust of rage and he spoke somewhat as follows: " I am ordered to proclaim *jihad*. A *jihad*, as you know, is a Holy War to protect our Holy Places against infidels. This being so, what are these infidel *pigs* doing in our mosque ? "

There was a most unseemly scuffle ; the Turco-

German contingent tried to seize the mullah; the Arab congregation defended him strenuously from arrest. In the confusion that worthy man got clear away and joined his family in Nejd. *Jihad* is incumbent on all Moslems if against infidel aggression. We stood on the defensive when the Turks first attacked us on the Canal, and when we finally overran Palestine and Syria it was in co-operation with the Arabs, who have more right there than the Turks.

Those who forged the blade of this counterfeit *jihad* could not temper it in the flame of religious fervour, and it shattered against the shield of religious tolerance and good faith: we make mistakes, but can honestly claim those two virtues.

CHAPTER III

ITS STRENGTH AND WEAKNESS

To gauge the strength or weakness of pan-Islam as a world-force we may best compare it with its great militant rival, the Christian Church, choosing common ground as the only sound basis of comparison, and remembering that it is pan-Islam we are examining rather than Islam itself—the tree, not the root; and though we cannot study the one without considering the other, Islam has already been extensively discussed by men better qualified than myself to deal with it: the requirements of this work only call for comparison so far as the driving-power of pan-Islam is concerned as a material force.

First of all we must discard common factors. I set the great Shiah schism against the Catholic Church (omitting the word "Roman" as a contradiction in terms) and cancel both for the purposes of comparison. Catholicism, is not, of course, schismatic, otherwise there are points of resemblance, such as observances of saints and shrines, which have permeated the other sects to a certain extent; also the degree of antagonism is about the same. Therefore we can ignore the Catholic Church in this chapter, and when we are talking of pan-Islam we should consider it a Sunnite (or Orthodox) movement, and count the Shiites out, as they do not even recognise the same centre of pilgrimage.

Perhaps the strongest factor in pan-Islam as a political movement or a world-wide fellowship is the Meccan pilgrimage. I have already alluded to its cosmopolitan nature in the previous chapter, but never realised it so much till after the surrender of Jeddah, when stately Bokhariots, jabbering Javanese, Malays, Chinese, Russians, American citizens and South Africans were among those who beset me as stranded pilgrims. This implies a very wide sphere of influence, against which we can only set the well-known immorality and greed which pilgrims complain of at Mecca; a huge influx of cosmopolitan visitors to *any* centre will generally cause such abuses. On the feast of Arafat there are normally 100,000 pilgrims in the Meccan area who represent 100 million orthodox Moslems throughout the world, while the actual population of the city is only 50,000.

The Arabic language is another strong bond of brotherhood in Islam. I do not mean to say that it is generally " understanded of the people," any more than Latin is throughout the Catholic world; but it is the language of most Sunnites and is moderately understood in Somaliland, East Africa, Java and the Malay peninsula as the language of the Koran; in fact, it is the only written language in Somaliland, and Turkey uses the script though not the tongue.

The daily observances of prayer, with their simple but obligatory ceremonial, and the yearly fast for the month of Ramadhan unite Moslems with the common ties of duty and hardship, as in the comradeship which sailors and soldiers have for each other throughout the world.

Then, again, there is no colour-line in Islam; a negro may rise to place and power (he often does), and usually enjoys the intimate confidence of his master as not readily amenable to local intrigue. Difference of nationality is not stressed except by the Young Turks, who have slighted Semitic Moslems to their own undoing. Contrast this attitude with our Church and estimate the precise amount of Christian brotherhood between an Orthodox Greek, a Welsh Wesleyan, an Ethiopian priest, a Scotch Presbyterian, and an Anglican bishop (since the Kikuyu heresy). Even within the narrow limits of one sect there is nothing like the fellowship one finds in secular societies. Which is the stronger appeal, "Anglican communicant" or "Freemason"? Is a cross or the quadrant and compasses the more potent charm?

Arabs credit us Christians with a much stronger bond of sympathy between co-religionists than is actually the case. It is true that those who come into any sort of contact with us realise that there is a distinct difference in form of worship and sentiment between Catholics (whom they call *Christyân*) and Protestants (or *Nasâra*), but I shall not readily forget the extraordinary conduct of a Hejazi who boarded us off Jeddah with some of the effects belonging to the murdered Germans mentioned in the previous chapter. He must have had the firm conviction that we Christians would avenge the killing of other Christians by Moslems, for he merely told me that he had in his possession certain property of the *Allemani*, and I told him that he would be suitably rewarded on producing it; I found out later that he had boasted to our ship's interpreter (a Mussulman) that he was one of the slayers, and it occurred to me that if that were the case he might be able to give me further information, or perhaps produce papers of theirs which might appear valueless to him but would be of interest to us. I interviewed him on deck and suggested this, reminding him of what he had told the interpreter, but laying no stress on the deed he had confessed, for it was outside our jurisdiction and no concern of mine.

"Papers?" he said. "By all means, I will go and fetch them," and breaking from my light hold of his sleeve he flickered over the rail and dropped into the sea some thirty feet below. Two armed marines stepped to the rail with a clatter of breech-bolts and looked inquiringly at me. Meanwhile my bold murderer was calling on his God, for he wore a full bandoleer, which was weighing him down. Out darted a fishing-canoe from under our quarter and made for him, but its occupants took the hint I conveyed through a megaphone and confined their efforts to saving him for the duty-cutter to pick up.

He was brought before me dripping wet, with the fear of death in his eyes. I thought this was due to the foolish risk he had taken, and spoke in gentle reproof of his conduct, pointing out that if any boat had been alongside where he leaped he would have met with a bad accident. To my surprise he fell at my feet and scrabbled at my clean white shoes, imploring me to spare his life. I put him down as somewhat mad, and asked "Number One" to put a sentry over him to see that he did not repeat his attempt to avoid our acquaintance. He clung to me like a limpet and had to be removed by force, with despairing entreaties for mercy, disregarding my still puzzled assurances as to his personal safety I learned afterwards his true reason for alarm ; he thought that after leaving my presence he would be quietly made away with in traditional Eastern style.

Another very strong feature of pan-Islam is the consistency of the creed from which it grows. I do not necessarily imply that Islam itself is benefited thereby, for consistency sometimes means narrowness, and we are not considering creeds ; but there is no doubt about the dynamic force of a movement based on a religion which is sure of itself. A Moslem has one authorised version of the Koran, and only one ; his simple creed is contained in its first chapter and is as short as the Lord's Prayer, which it somewhat resembles in style. Praising God as the Lord of the worlds (not only of this world of ours), it attributes to Him mercy and clemency with supreme power over the Day of Judgment and is an avowal of worship and service. Its only petition is to be led in the way of the righteous, avoiding errors that incur His wrath. Contrast this with the many confusing aspects of Christianity. Perhaps diverse opinions tend to purify and invigorate a creed, but they certainly do not strengthen the cohesion of any secular movement based on it.

Then, again, the Moslem conception of God and the hereafter stiffens the backbone of pan-Islam in adversity. They are taught to believe that He is *really* omnipotent and that His actions are beyond criticism—welfare and affliction being alike acceptable as His will. We, on the other hand, seem to be developing the theory of a finite God warring against, and occasionally overcome by, evil, which includes (in this new thesis) human suffering and sorrow as well as sin. There is a growing idea, pioneered partly by Mr. H. G. Wells and apparently supported by many of the clergy, that the acts of God must square with human ideals of mercy or justice, and as many occurrences do not, the inference is that evil gets the best of it sometimes. Now the Moslem slogan is "Allah Akbar" (God is Greatest), and that seems to me a better battle-cry than, for example, "Gott mit uns," as God will still be great and invincible to Moslems in their victory or defeat; but the finite idea presumes, in disaster, that you and your God have been defeated together. It is not my business to criticise either conception from a religious point of view, but in mundane affairs it is the former that will make for fighting force, especially as we still insist that our God is a jealous God, visiting the sins of the fathers, etc.: surely this is not a human ideal of justice; the obvious deduction is that our modern Deity is stronger to punish than protect—hardly an encouraging attribute.

Whether a religion is the better for an organised priesthood or not is irrelevant to our subject, but the absence of it in Islam certainly strengthens the pan-Islamic movement, as each Moslem may consider himself a standard-bearer of his faith, while we are apt to leave too much to our priests, thus engendering slackness on our part and meticulous dogma on theirs; both undermine Christian brotherhood. The fact that priestly stipends seem to the ordinary layman as in inverse ratio to the duties performed also widens the breach between clergy and laity, besides sapping clerical *moral*. This is not the particular feature of any one sect—the reader can supply cases within his own experience, but here is one that is probably outside it and showing how wide-spread the system is. The rank and file of the Greek Orthodox clergy are notoriously ill-paid. Yet their monastery at Jerusalem costs £E.15,000 per annum to maintain and pays £E.40,000 annually in clerical salaries to archbishops and clergy who control the spiritual affairs of less than fifteen thousand people. It derives £E.30,000 from its property in Russia, £E.25,000 from the property of the Holy Sepulchre, and as much again from visitors and other sources; and this in a region where the Founder of our faith was content to wander with less certainty of shelter than the wild creatures of the countryside.

Incidentally, the monastery seems to have been unable to curtail its expenditure during the War, for it has accumulated debts to the amount of £E.600,000, most of its sources of income having ceased for the time. I quote from current newspapers. Blame does not necessarily attach to the monastery or its administrators, who may have done their best to fulfil their obligations under adverse circumstances; I would merely draw attention to the incongruity of the whole system as regards a universal brotherhood based on Christian teaching. There are no such exotic growths to impede the march of pan-Islam.

So much for the strength of the pan-Islamic movement. Now let us consider its weak points.

To begin with, the gross abuse of pan-Islam by interested parties for non-spiritual ends during the War has done the genuine movement harm. That lying, political appeal to *jihad* has made thinking Moslems mistrust the infallibility of organised pan-Islam, of which the culminating expression is Holy War, one of the most sacred Mussulman duties if justly invoked. We Christians do not make such mistakes. When Italy was fighting the Turks in Tripoli the Pope himself warned Christian soldiers against regarding the campaign as a Crusade, and when we took Jerusalem we took it side by side with our Mussulman allies and forthwith placed an orthodox Moslem guard on Omar's mosque. In this connection it may be of interest to note that the officer commanding a mixed Christian guard at the Holy Sepulchre was a Jew.

Another source of weakness, so far as a united Moslem world is concerned, may be found in the antagonistic points of view between civilised and uncivilised Moslems (I use the attribute in its modern sense). Uncivilised Moslems view with suspicion and, in fact, derision the dress and customs of their civilised co-religionists, insisting that European coats and trousers display the figure indecently and that their Frankish luxuries and amusements are snares of Eblis. The enlightened Moslem, on the other hand, regards the tribesman as a *jungliwala*, or wild man of the woods, derides his illiteracy, and is revolted by the harsh severity of the old Islamic penal code as practised still in semi-barbaric Moslem States.

Now we Christians are fairly lenient as regards each other's customs, and still more so with regard to dress (judging by the garb we tolerate), while we have quite outgrown our old playful habits of boiling, burning, or torturing our fellow-men except on the battle-fields of civilised warfare.

Civilisation (as we understand it) is a two-edged weapon and tool smiting or serving pan-Islam and Christendom, but on the whole it serves the latter rather than the former, as the superior resources of Christendom can take fuller advantage of it as a tool or a weapon, though both turn to scourges when used against each other in battle. Also its handmaid, Education, though in itself a foe to no religion, *does* tend to tone down dogma and engender tolerance, thus minimising the dynamic force of bigotry in pan-Islam, though consolidating the real stability of religion on its own base. Moreover, some gifts of civilisation can do a lot of harm if wrongly used; I refer more especially to drink, drugs, and dress. Just as hereditary exposure to the infection of certain diseases is said to confer, by survival of the fittest, a certain immunity therefrom—for example, consumption among us Europeans and typhoid among Asiatics—so moral ills seem to affect humanity to a greater or less extent in inverse proportion to the temptation in that particular respect which the individual and his forebears have successfully resisted. The average European and his ancestors have been accustomed to drink fermented liquor for many centuries, and in moderation as judged by the standard of his time, but he has always been taught to avoid opium and has not known the drug for long. The oriental Moslem, on the other hand, has used opium as a remedy and prophylactic against malaria for generations, but is strictly ordered by his creed to consider the consumption, production, gift or sale of alcohol a deadly sin. In consequence, the European can usually take alcohol in moderation, but almost invariably slips into a pit of his own digging when he tries to do the same with opium, while the oriental Moslem can use opium in moderation (provided that he confines himself to swallowing it and does not smoke it), but when he drinks, usually drinks to excess because he has not learned to do otherwise. It is a melancholy fact that hitherto in countries opened up by our Western civilisation drink has got in long before education, unless extraordinary precautions have been taken to prevent it; that is one reason why Moslem States are so wary of civilised encroachment. As for drugs other than opium (and far more dangerous), civilised Moslems, especially in Egypt, are alarmed at the spread of hashish-smoking among their co-religionists, while the cultured classes, including women-folk, are taking to cocaine: the material for both vices is supplied from European sources, mostly Greek. Dress, compared with the other two demons, is merely a fantastic though mischievous sprite and can be quite attractive, but it breaks up many a Moslem home when carried to excess in the harem, as it frequently is in civilised circles, while the younger men vie with each other in the more flagrant extravagances of occidental garb: prayers and ablutions do not harmonise with well-creased trousers and stylish boots any more than a veil does with a divided skirt. The native Press is always attacking the above abuses, but they are firmly rooted. All three undermine the pan-Islamic structure by causing cleavage in public opinion. European dress has already been mentioned as widening the gap between civilised and uncivilised Moslems, but it also tends to disintegrate cultured Moslem communities, for the older men are apt to regard it with suspicion or downright condemnation. I once asked an eminent and learned Moslem whether he thought modern European dress impeded regular observance of prayers and ablutions. He replied, "Perhaps so, but those

Moslems who wear such clothes indicate by so doing that the observances of Islam have little hold upon them."

All these defects, however, are mere cracks in the inner walls of the pan-Islamic structure and can be repaired from within, but the Turkish Government, which represented the Caliphate, and should have considered the integrity of Islam as a sacred trust, has managed to split the outer wall and divide the house against itself, just as the unity of Christendom (such as it was) has been rent asunder by one of its most prominent exponents. Pan-Islam has received the more serious damage because the wreckers still hold the Caliphate and the prestige attached thereto; it is for Moslems (and Moslems only) to decide what action to take; but in any case, the breach is a serious one and has been much widened by the action of Turkish troops at the Holy Places. They actually shelled the Caaba at Mecca (luckily without doing material damage), and their action in storing high explosives close to the Prophet's tomb at Medina may have saved them bombardment, but has certainly not improved their reputation as Moslems. Even before the War I often heard Yamen Arabs talking of "Turks and Moslems"—a distinctly damning discrimination—and the situation has not been improved by Ottoman slackness in religious observances and their inconsistent national movement.

At the same time, their rule in Arabia will be awkward to replace at first. I described the Turks in the final chapter of a book * published early in the War as pre-eminently fitted to govern Moslems by birthright, creed, and temperament, summing them up as individually gifted but collectively hopeless as administrators because they lacked a stable and consistent central Government. They have proved the indictment up to the hilt, but that does not dower any of us Christians with their inherent qualifications as rulers in Islam. If any of us are called upon to face fresh responsibilities in this direction, it would take us all our time to make up for these qualities by tact, sound administration, and strict observance of local religious prejudice. Even then there is a Mussulman proverb to this effect: "A Moslem ruler though he oppress me and not a *kafir* though he work me weal"—it explains much apparent ingratitude for benefits conferred.

The lesson we have to learn from pan-Islamic activities of the last decade or two is that countries which are mainly Moslem should have Moslem rulers, and that Christian rule, however enlightened and benevolent, is only permissible where Islam

* "*Arabia Infelix*," Macmillan.

is outnumbered by other creeds. At the same time, in countries where Christian methods of civilisation and European capital have been invited we have a right to control and advise the Moslem ruler sufficiently to ensure the fair treatment of our nationals and their interests. But with purely Moslem countries which have expressed no readiness to assimilate the methods of modern civilisation or to invite outside capital we have no right to interfere beyond the following limit: if the local authorities allow foreign traders to operate at their ports their interests should be safeguarded, if important enough, by consular representation on the spot, or, if not, by occasional visits of a man-of-war to keep nationals in touch with their own Government, presuming that the place is too small to justify any mail-carrying vessel calling there except at very long intervals.

There should always be a definite understanding as to foreigners proceeding or residing up-country for any purpose. If the local ruler discourages but permits such procedure, all we should expect him to do in case of untoward incidents is to take reasonable action to investigate and punish, but if he has guaranteed the security of foreign nationals concerned, he must redeem his pledge in an adequate manner or take the consequences.

There should seldom be occasion for an inland punitive expedition; in these days, when many articles of seaborne trade have become, from mere luxuries, almost indispensable adjuncts of native life in the remotest regions, a maritime blockade strictly enforced should soon exact the necessary satisfaction.

Such rulers should bear in mind that if they accept an enterprise of foreign capital they must protect its legitimate operations, just as a school which has accepted a Government grant has to conform to stipulated conditions.

Where no such penetration has occurred, all we should concern ourselves with is that internal trouble in such regions shall not slop over into territory protected or occupied by us, and this is where our most serious difficulties will occur in erstwhile Turkish Arabia.

The Turk, with all his faults, could grapple with a difficult situation in native affairs by drastic methods which might be indefensible in themselves, but were calculated to obtain definite results. At any rate, we had a responsible central Government to deal with and one that we could get at. Now we shall have to handle such situations ourselves or rely on the local authorities doing so. The former method is costly and dangerous, yielding the minimum of result to the maximum of effort and expense, while involving possibilities of trouble which might compromise our democratic yearnings considerably: the latter alternative presupposes that we have succeeded in evolving out of the present imbroglio responsible rulers who are well-disposed to us and prepared to take adequate action on our representations.

In Syria and Mesopotamia, where communications are good and European penetration an established fact, there should not be much difficulty, but in Arabia proper the problem is a very prickly one.

Beginning with Arabia Felix, which includes Yamen, the Aden protectorate, and the vague, sprawling province of Hadhramaut, we may be permitted to hope that nothing worse can happen in the Aden protectorate than has happened already; the remoter Hadhramaut has always looked after its own affairs and can continue to do so; but Yamen bristles with political problems which will have to be solved, and solved correctly, if she is going to be a safe neighbour or a reliable customer to have business dealings with. Hitherto none of her local rulers have inspired any confidence in their capacity for initiative or independent action. During the War the Idrisi, who had long been in revolt against the Turks in northern Yamen, kept making half-hearted and abortive dabs at Loheia—like a nervous child playing snapdragon—but his only success (and temporary at that) was when he occupied the town after the Red Sea Patrol had shelled the Turks out of it. As for the Imam, he has been sitting on a very thorny fence ever since the Turks came into the War. We have been in touch with him for a long time, but all he has done up to date is to wobble on a precarious tripod supported by the opposing strains of Turks, tribesmen, and British. Now one leg of the tripod has been knocked away he has yet to show if he can maintain stability on his own base, and, if so, over what area. The undeniable fighting qualities of the Yamen Arab, which might be a useful factor in a stable government, will merely prove a nuisance and a menace under a weak *régime*, and tribal trouble will always be slopping over into our Aden sphere of influence. Then the question will arise, What are we going to do about it? We cannot bring the Yamenis to book by blockading their coast and cutting off caravan traffic with Aden, because, in view of our trade relations with the country by sea and land, we should only be cutting our nose off to spite our face. Moreover, the punishment would fall chiefly on the respectable community.

traders, the cultured classes, etc., to whom sea-borne trade is essential, while it would hardly affect the wild tribesmen, except as regards ammunition, and to prevent them getting what they wanted through the Hejaz is outside the sphere of practical politics.

In the Hejaz itself we can at least claim that authority is suitably represented and accessible to us. Before the War we kept a British consul at Jeddah with an Indian Moslem vice-consul who went up to Mecca in the pilgrim season. A responsible consular agent (Moslem of course) to reside at Medina, also another to understudy the Jeddah vice-consul when he went to Mecca and to look after the Yenbo pilgrim traffic, would safeguard the interests of our nationals, who enormously outnumber the pilgrims of any other nation. Further interference with the Hejaz, unless invited, would be unjustifiable.

Trouble for us does not lie in the Hejaz itself, but in its possible expansion beyond its powers of absorption, or, in homely metaphor, if it bites off more than it can chew There is a certain tendency just now to overrate Hejazi prowess in war and policy; in fact, King Husein is often alluded to vaguely as the "King of Arabia," and there is a sporadic crop of ill-informed articles on this and other Arabian affairs in the English Press. One of the features of the War as regards this part of the world is the extraordinary and fungus-like growth of "Arabian experts" it has produced, most of whom have never set foot in Arabia itself, while the few now living who have acquired real first-hand knowledge of any part of the Arabian peninsula before the War may be counted on the fingers of one hand. Yet the number of people who rush into print with their opinions on the most complex Arabian affairs would astonish even the Arabs if they permitted themselves to show surprise at anything. These opinions differ widely, but have one attribute in common—their emphatic "cock-sureness." Each one presents the one and only solution of the whole Arabian problem according to the facet which the writer has seen, and there are many facets. They are amusing and even instructive occasionally, but there is a serious side to them—their crass empiricism. Each writer presents (quite honestly, perhaps) his point of view of one or two facets in the rough-cut, many-sided and clouded crystal of Arabian politics without considering its possible bearing on other parts of the peninsula or even other factors in the district he knows or has read about. The net result is an appallingly crude patchwork, no one piece harmonising with another, and, in view of the habit Government has formed in these cases of accepting empirical opinions if they are shouted loud enough or at close range, there is more than a possibility that our Arabian policy may resemble such a crazy quilt. If it does, we shall have to harvest a thistle-crop of tribal and intertribal trouble throughout the Arabian peninsula, and the seed-down of unrest will blow all over Syria and Mesopotamia just at the most awkward time when reconstruction and sound administration are struggling to establish themselves. Weeds grow quicker and stronger than useful plants in any garden.

Empirical statements sound well and look well in print, but they are no use whatever as sailing directions in the uncharted waters of Arabian politics. Putting them aside, the following facts are worth bearing in mind when the future of Arabia is discussed.

The Hejazi troops were ably led by the Sharifian Emirs and Syrian officers of note, and had the co-operation of the Red Sea flotilla on the coast and British officers of various corps inland to cut off Medina, the last place of importance held by the Turks after the summer of 1916. Yet the town held out until long after the armistice, and its surrender had eventually to be brought about by putting pressure on the Turkish Government at Stamboul. On the other hand, the two great provinces which impinge upon the Hejaz, namely, Nejd and Yamen, have given ample proof that they can hammer the Turks without outside assistance. The Nejdis not only cleared their own country of Ottoman rule, but drove the Turks out of Hasa a year or two before the War, while the Yamenis have more than once hurled the Turks back on to the coast, and the rebels of northern Yamen successfully withstood a Hejazi and Turkish column from the north and another Turkish column from the south. The inference is that if the limits of Hejazi rule are to be much extended there had better be a clear understanding with their neighbours and also some definite idea of the extent to which we are likely to be involved in support of our *protégé*.

I know that many otherwise intelligent people have been hypnotised by the prophecy in "The White Prophet":

> "The time is near when the long drama that has been played between Arabs and Turks will end in the establishment of a vast Arabic empire, extending from the Tigris and the Euphrates valley to the Mediterranean and from the Indian Ocean to Jerusalem, with Cairo as its Capital, the Khedive as its Caliph, and England as its lord and protector."

While refraining from obvious and belated

criticism of a prophecy which the march of events has trodden out of shape, and which could never have been intended as a serious contribution to our knowledge of Arabs and their politics, we must admit that the basic idea of centralising Arabian authority has taken strong hold of avowed statecraft in England. It would, of course, simplify our relations with Arabia and the collateral regions of Mesopotamia and Syria if such authority could establish itself and be accepted by the other Arabian provinces to the extent of enforcing its enactments as regards their foreign affairs, *i.e.*, relations with subjects (national or protected) of European States.

If such authority could be maintained without assistance from us other than a subsidy and the occasional supply, to responsible parties, of arms and ammunition, it would satisfy all reasonable requirements, but if we had to intervene with direct force we should find ourselves defending an unpopular *protégé* against the united resentment of Arabia.

I believe there is no one ruler or ruling clique in Arabia that could wield such authority, and my reason for saying so is that the experiment has been tried repeatedly on a small scale during the twenty years or so that I have been connected with the country and has failed every time. Toward the close of last century a sultan of Lahej who had always claimed suzerainty over his turbulent neighbours, the Subaihi, had to enter that vagabond tribeship to enforce one of his decrees, and got held up with his "army" until extricated by Aden diplomacy at the price of his suzerain sway. His successor still claimed a hold over an adjacent clan of the Subaihi known as the Rigai, but when one of our most promising political officers was murdered there, and the murderer sheltered by the clan, he was unable to obtain redress or even assist us adequately in attempting to do so. Early in this century Aden was involved in a little expedition against Turks and Arabs because one of her protected sultans (equipped with explosive and ammunition) could not deal with a small Arab fort himself. This is the same sultanate which let the Turks through against us in the summer of 1915 and whose ruler was prominent in the sacking of Lahej. I have already alluded, in Chapter II, to the inadequacy of the Lahej sultan on that occasion, yet Aden had bolstered up his authority in every possible way and had relied on him and his predecessor for years to act as semi-official suzerain and go-between for other tribes—a withered stick which snapped the first time it was leant upon. I could also point to the Imam of Yamen, strong in opposition to the Turks as a rallying point of tribal revolt, but weak and vacillating on the side of law and order. I might go on giving instances *ad nauseam*, but here is one more to clinch the argument, and it is typical of Arab politics. Aden had just cause of offence against a certain reigning sultan of the Abd-ul-Wahid in her eastern sphere of influence. He had intrigued with foreign States, oppressed his subjects, persecuted native trade and played the dickens generally. Therefore Aden rebuked him (by letter) and appointed a relative of his to be sultan and receive his subsidy. The erring but impenitent potentate reduced his relative to such submission that he would sign monthly receipts for the subsidy and meekly hand over the cash: these were his only official acts, as he retired into private life in favour of Aden's *bête noir*, who flourished exceedingly until he blackmailed caravans too freely and got the local tribesmen on his track.

When we also consider how early in Islamic history the Caliphate split as a temporal power, and the difficulty which even the early Caliphs (with all their prestige) had to keep order in Arabia, it should engender caution in experiments toward even partial centralisation of control: apart from the fact that they might develop along lines diverging from the recognised principles of self-determination in small States, they could land us into a humiliating *impasse* or an armed expedition.

We parried the Turco-German efforts to turn pan-Islam against us, thanks to our circumspect attitude with regard to Moslems, but a genuine movement based on any apparent aggression of ours in Arabia proper might be a more serious matter.

CHAPTER IV

MOSLEM AND MISSIONARY

HAVING weighed the influence which pan-Islam can wield as a popular movement, we will now consider the human factors which have built it up.

Just as we used Christendom as a test-gauge of pan-Islam, so now we will compare the activities of Moslems (who do their own proselytising) with those of Christian missionaries, grouping with them our laity so far as their example may be placed in the scales for or against the influence of Christendom.

To do this with the breadth of view which the question demands we will examine these human factors throughout the world wherever they are involved in opposition to each other. We shall thus avoid the confined outlook which teaches Europeans in Asia Minor to look on Turks as typical Moslems to the exclusion of all others, or makes Anglo-Egyptians talk of country-folk in Egypt as Arabs and their language as the standard of Arabic, or engenders the Anglo-Indian tendency of regarding a scantily-dressed paramount chief from the Aden hinterland as an obscure *jungli-wala* because, in civilised India, an eminent Moslem dresses in accordance with our conception of the part.

We can leave the western hemisphere out of this inquiry, for though the greatest missionary effort against Islam is engendered in the United States, it manifests itself in the eastern hemisphere, and the Moslem population in both the Americas is too small and quiescent to be considered a factor.

We will begin with England and work eastward to the edge of the Moslem world.

At first glance the idea of England as an arena where two great religious forces meet seems rather far-fetched, but there is more Moslem activity in some of our English towns than people imagine. Turning over some files of the *Kibla* (a Meccan newspaper), one comes across passages like the following :—

"The honourable Cadi Abdulla living in London reports that six noted English men and women have embraced the Moslem religion in the cities of Oxford, Leicester, etc. The meritorious Abdul Hay Arab has established a new centre in London for calling to Islam, and the Mufti Muhammad Sadik has delivered a speech in English in the mosque on 'the object of human life which can only be attained through Moslem guidance.' Many English men and women were present and put questions which were answered in a conclusive manner. At the close of the meeting a young lady of good family embraced Islam and was named Maimuna."

Then we have the scholarly and temperate addresses of Seyid Muhammad Rauf and others before the Islamic Society in London; they are marked by considerable shrewdness and breadth of view, and though their debatable points may present a few fallacies, their effective controversion requires unusual knowledge of affairs in Moslem countries.

It is not, however, the activities of Moslems in England which damage the prestige of Christendom; it is the behaviour of English alleged Christians themselves. Every missionary, political officer, tutor, or even the importer of a native servant—in short, anyone who has been responsible for an oriental in England—knows what I mean. I do not say that London (for example) is any more vicious than Delhi or Cairo or Cabul or Constantinople or any other large Moslem centre, but vice is certainly more obvious in London to the casual observer, even allowing for the fact that many comparatively harmless customs of ours (such as women wearing low-necked dresses and dancing with men) are apt to shock Moslems until they learn that occidental habit has created an atmosphere of innocence in such cases which even bunny-hugging has failed to vitiate.

The social life of London in all its grades and phases operates more widely for good or ill on Christian prestige among Moslems than Londoners can possibly imagine. From the young princeling of some native State sauntering about Club-land with his bear-leader to the lascar off a P. and O. boat, among East London drabs, or the middle-class Mohammedan student who compares the civic achievements that surround him with the dingy dining-room of a Bloomsbury boarding-house, all are apostles of life in London as it seems to them. I have had the hospitality of "family hotels" in the Euston Road portrayed to me in the crude but vivid imagery of the East when spooring boar in Southern Morocco with a native tracker who had been one of a troupe of Soosi jugglers earning good pay at a West-end music-hall, and I once overheard a young *effendi* explaining to his *confrères* in a Cairo café exactly the sort of company that would board your hansom when leaving "Jimmy's" in days of yore.

As for the news of London and its ways, as conveyed by its daily Press, educated Egyptians were better posted therein than most Englishmen in Cairo during the War, as their clubs and private organisations subscribed largely to the London dailies, which entered Egypt free of local censorship, while Anglo-Egyptian newspapers were more strictly censored than their vernacular or continental contemporaries, as they presented no linguistic difficulties, but could be dealt with direct and not through an understrapper.

Missionaries would have us judge Islam by the open improprieties and abuses which occur at Mecca, Kerbela, and other great Moslem centres. How should we like Christianity to be judged by the public behaviour of certain classes in London or other big towns? Remember, it is always the scum which floats on top and the superficial vice or indecorum that strike a foreign observer.

It is not my mission to preach—I am merely pointing out a flaw in our harness which causes a lot of administrative trouble out East. It is difficult to check the hashish habit in Egypt when the average educated *effendi* reads of drug-scandals in London with mischievous avidity, and the endeavours of a well-meaning Education Department to implant ideals of sturdy manhood are handicapped when the students batten on the weird and unsavoury incidents which are dished up *in extenso* by London journalism from time to time. Such matters do no harm to a public with a sense of proportion, but the *effendi* is in the position of a schoolboy who has caught his master tripping and means to make the most of it. He assimilates and disseminates the idea that cocaine is as easily procurable as a cocktail in London clubs, and that the Black Mass is at least as common as the *danse de ventre* in Cairo.

We can leave England for our Eastern tour with the conclusion that Islam is welcome to any proselytes it makes there, but that the gravest slur on Christian prestige is cast by our own conduct.

There is only one bone of contention between Moslems and missionaries in Europe now that Turkey and Russia are knocked out of the ring of current politics. Is St. Sophia to remain a mosque or revert to its original purpose as a Christian church? Whatever may be Turkish opinion on the subject, the tradition of Islam is definite enough. When the Caliph Omar entered Jerusalem in triumph, after Khaled had defeated the hosts of Heraclius east of Jordan, he withstood the importunate entreaties of his followers to pray in the Church of the Holy Sepulchre, saying that if he did so the building would *de facto* become a mosque, and such a wrong to Christianity was against the ordinance and procedure of the Prophet. It is worthy of note that Christians were not molested at Jerusalem until after the Seljouk Turks wrested the Holy City from the moribund Arabian Caliphate in 1076: their persecution and the desecration of sacred places by the Turks brought about the first Crusade in 1096. Again it was the Ottoman Turks who stormed Constantinople and turned St. Sophia into a mosque. According to the orthodox tradition of Islam, once a church always a church. When the ex-Khedive had the chance of re-acquiring the site of All Saints', Cairo, owing to the increasing noise of traffic in the vicinity, he contemplated building a cinema-theatre there (for he had a shrewd business mind), but he was roundly told by Moslem legalists that it was out of the question. Even if the Turks urge right of conquest, victorious Christendom can claim that too, and if they allege length of tenure as a mosque in support of their case they put themselves out of court, as St. Sophia has been a church for more than nine centuries and a mosque for less than five.

If Turkey is allowed to remain in Europe at all it will be on sufferance. Even in Asia Minor signs are not wanting that Turkish rule will be pruned, clipped and trained considerably, as humanity will stand its rampant luxuriance of blood and barbarity no longer. The Young

Turks were given every chance to consolidate their national aspirations and have achieved national suicide. One may feel sorry for the patient, sturdy peasantry and the non-political cultured classes who have been coerced or cajoled into fighting desperately in a cause that meant calamity for them whether they won or lost; but a nation gets the rulers it deserves and must answer for their acts.

Asia Minor will probably be more accessible as a mission-field in due course. The Moslem Turk is not amenable to conversion; in fact, during a quarter of a century's wandering in the East I have never met a Turkish convert. The American Protestant Mission will probably be well to the fore in this area in view of its excellent work on behalf of the Armenians and other distressed Christians during the War. Just as it has concentrated its principal energies on the Copts in Egypt, so it may with advantage devote itself to the education and "uplift" of the Armenians, and if its activities are as successful as with the Copts, even the Armenians cannot but approve, for the more enlightened individuals of that harassed and harassing little nation admit that the Armenian character could be considerably improved, and that, though their hideous persecution is indefensibly damnable, their covetous instincts and parasitic activities are an incentive to maltreatment.

One of the most difficult minor problems of reconstruction in Eastern Europe and Asia Minor will be how to safeguard the interests and modify the provocative activities of such subject-races as the Jews and the Armenians where established among ill-controlled nations and numerically inferior, though intellectually superior, to them. With their natural gift for intrigue and finance, they repay public persecution and oppression by undermining the administration and battening on the resources of their unwilling foster-country until active dislike becomes actual violence and outbursts of brutish rage yield ghastly results. Deportation is not only tyrannically harsh but impracticable, for unless they were dumped to die in the waste places of the earth, which is unthinkable, some other nation must receive them, and even the most philanthropic Government would hesitate to upset its economic conditions by admitting unproductive hordes of sweated labour and skilled exploiters. There are only two logical alternatives to such an *impasse*. One is to treat such subject-races so well that they may be trusted not to use their peculiar abilities against the interests of their adoptive country, which would then be their interests too, and the other is to exterminate them, which is inhuman. There is no middle course.

It is a salutary but humiliating fact that we incur the worst human ills by our lack of human charity. We starved and overcrowded our poor till they bred consumption, and we enslaved negroes till they degenerated our Anglo-Saxon sturdiness of character, then plunged a great nation into civil war, and have finally become one of its most serious social problems. So the Jews were debarred from liberal pursuits and privileges until they concentrated on finance and commerce, being also persecuted until they perfected their defensive organisation. The consequence is that they are individually formidable in those activities and collectively invincible. Similarly the Turks harried the Armenians to their own undoing with even less excuse, for those ill-used people were certainly not interlopers, and so far from ameliorating their condition in the course of time, as we have done with the Jews, the Turks went from bad to worse till they culminated in atrocities which no provocation can palliate or humanity condone.

But to return to Asia Minor; there the Armenians were first on the ground, and yet the Moslems of Armenia outnumber them by three to one. Any sound form of government would have to give equal rights, but it would have to be strong and farseeing to prevent the greedy exploitation and savage reprisals which such conditions would otherwise evolve.

On entering Asia we shall find a somewhat similar problem confronting the administration in Syria and Palestine. Here we have several mixed races and at least three distinct creeds—Christianity, Islam, and Judaism.

The Zionist movement looks promising, everyone concerned seems to be in accord, and a Jew millennium looms large in the offing, but ——. In Palestine there are normally about 700,000 Moslems and Christians (the latter a very small minority) to 150,000 Jews. The lure of the Promised Land will presumably increase the Jewish population enormously, but they will still be very much in the minority unless the country is over-populated. The Zionist organisation will naturally try to select for emigration agriculturists, mechanics, and craftsmen generally to develop the resources of the country, but that is easier said than done. If Palestine, in addition to the sentimental aspect, is to be a refuge and asylum for the downtrodden and persecuted Jews of Eastern Europe, there would be very few farmers among *that* lot — except tax-farmers. Even in England, where he labours under no landowning disability, the Jew thinks that farming for a living is a mug's game and confines his agricultural activities to week-ends in the autumn with a "hammerless ejector" and a knickerbocker suit. As for mechanics and skilled labour generally, such Jews as take to it usually excel in such work and do very well where they are. The bulk of the immigrant population—unless Palestine is going to be artificially colonised without regard for the necessitous claims of the very people who should be drawn off there—will be indigent artisans, small shopkeepers, shop assistants, weedy unemployables, and a sprinkling of shrewd operators on the look-out for prey. If the scheme is going to be run entirely on philanthropic lines (and there are ample resources and charity at the back of it to do so) the Zionists will be all right, and will, perhaps, improve immensely in the next generation under the influence of an open-air life—if they adopt it; but the resident majority of Moslems and Christians will not take too kindly to their new compatriots, while the Palestine Jews are already carping at the idea of so many trade rivals and accusing them of not being orthodox. None of this ill-feeling need matter in the long run with a firm but benevolent government, but the authorities will have to evolve some legislation to check profiteering and over-exploitation, or there will be trouble. It is not only the new-comers who will want curbing, but the present population. During the War the flagrant profiteering of Jew and Christian operators in Palestine and Syria did much to accentuate the appalling distress and was the more disgraceful compared with the magnificent efforts of the American and Anglican Churches to relieve the situation. The Jews nearly incurred a pogrom by their operations, which were only checked by a wealthy Syrian in Egypt starting a co-operative venture of low-priced foodstuffs and necessities with the support of the British authorities. As for the local Syrians, some of them were even worse. French and British officers speak of wealthy Syrians (presumably Christian, certainly not Moslem) giving many and sumptuous balls at Beyrout, at which they lapped Austrian champagne while their wives, blazing in diamonds, whirled with Hunnish officers in the high-pressure, double-action German waltz. And this with thousands of their compatriots starving in the streets and little naked children banding together to drive pariah dogs with stones from the street offal they were worrying, if perchance it might yield a meal. Meanwhile decent Anglo-

Saxon Christendom was battling in that very town under adverse conditions to succour human destitution which had been largely caused by the callous operations of these soulless parasites. The Christians of Syria have no monopoly of such scandals. Yet there are otherwise intelligent people who speak of modern Christianity as an automatic promoter of ethics, and have the effrontery to try to thrust it on the East as a moral panacea. It is human ideals which make or mar a soul when once the seed of any sound religion has been sown, and they depend upon environment and climate more than our spiritual pastors admit; otherwise, why this missionary activity among oriental Christians? If you try to grow garden flowers in the rich, rank irrigation soil of the Nile valley they flourish luxuriantly, but soon develop a marked tendency to revert to their wild type, and it is permissible to suppose that human character is even more sensitive to its mental and physical surroundings. Any observant teacher of oriental youth will tell you that the promise of their precocious ability is seldom fulfilled by their maturity. Even the "country-born" children of British parents are considered precocious at their preparatory school in England, and, if not sent home to be educated, are apt to fall short of their parents' intellectual and moral standard in later years. The Mamelukes knew what they were about when they kidnapped hardy Albanian youths to carry on their rule in Egypt and passed over their own progeny. Kingsley has shown us in "Hypatia" what the Nile valley did for the Christian Church.

It is not a question of Jew, Christian, or Moslem that the administrative authorities in Syria and Palestine will have to consider beyond ensuring that each shall follow his religion unmolested. They will have to defend the many from the machinations of the few and the few from the violent reprisals of the many. It is statecraft that is wanted, not politics or religious dogma.

In Mesopotamia there has not been much missionary effort hitherto, and there is not a good case for exploiting it as a missionary field beyond certain limits. The riparian townsfolk are respectable people of some education and grasp of their own affairs, and the country-folk are a harum-scarum set of scallywags who used to attack Turks or British indifferently, whichever happened to be in difficulties for the moment. They are best left to the secular arm for some time to come. Medical missions, staffed by both sexes, could do good work at urban centres, and a few river steamers, or even launches, would extend their efforts considerably.

We now come to Arabia itself, "the Peninsula of the Arabs," where orthodox Islam has its strongholds and missionary enterprise is not encouraged.

Geographers differ somewhat as to what constitutes Arabia proper, but for the purposes of modern practical politics it may be considered as all the peninsula south of a line from the head of the Gulf of Akaba to the head of the Persian Gulf, and consisting of Nejd, the Hejaz,* Asir, Yamen, Aden protectorate, Hadhramaut and Oman. Each of these divisions should be dealt with separately in considering Arabian politics nowadays, and it will be well for the "mandatories" concerned if further sub-divisions do not complicate matters; I omit the sub-province of Hasa (once a dependency of the Turkish *pashalik* at Bussora) because, since the Nejdi *coup d'état* in 1912, the Emir ibn Saoud will probably control its policy *vis-à-vis* of missionaries and Europeans generally, though the Sheikh of Koweit may expect to be consulted.

Nejd comes first as we move southward:

* The definite article precedes most Arabic place-names, but is only retained in ordinary local speech as above, presumably to denote respect. I hold to native pronunciation, except in cases of long-established custom, and consider "the Yamen" as clumsy as "the Egypt"—both take the definite article in Arabian script

impinging as it does on Syria, Mesopotamia, and the Hejaz, its politics are involved in theirs to a certain extent and its affairs require careful handling. It is certainly no field for unrestrained missionary effort, but there is no reason why a medical mission should not be posted at Riadh if the Emir is willing. There are two rival houses in Nejd—the ibn Saoud and ibn Rashid, the former pro-British and the latter (hitherto) pro-Turk; Emir Saoud held ascendancy before the War and should be able to maintain it now that Turco-German influence is a thing of the past. He is an enlightened, energetic man and was a close friend of our gallant "political," the late Captain Shakespeare, who was killed there early in the War during an engagement between the two rival houses. The question of missionary enterprise in Nejd could well be put before the Emir for consideration on its merits. Such procedure may seem weak to an out-and-out missionary, but even he would hesitate to keep poultry in another man's garden, even for economic purposes, without consulting him. Fowls and missionaries are useful and even desirable in a suitable environment, otherwise they can be a nuisance.

Next in order as we travel is the Hejaz, where Islam started on its mission to harry exotic creeds and nations, until its conquering progress was checked decisively by reinvigorated Christendom. In missionary parlance, Arabia generally is referred to as "a Gibraltar of fanaticism and pride which shuts out the messenger of Christ," and it must be admitted that the Hejaz has hitherto justified this description to a certain extent. Even at Jeddah Christians were only just tolerated before the War, and I found it advisable, when exploring its tortuous bazars, to wear a tarboosh, which earned me the respectful salutations then accorded to a Turk. The indigenous townsfolk of Jeddah are the "meanest" set of Moslems I have ever met—I use the epithet in its American sense, as indicating a blend of currishness and crabbedness. They cringed to the Turk when the braver Arabs of the south were hammering the oppressor in Asir and Yamen, but, like pariahs, were ready to fall on them and their women and children when they had surrendered after a gallant struggle, overwhelmed by an intensive bombardment from the sea. The alien Moslems resident in Jeddah—especially the Indians—are not a bad lot, but there is an atmosphere of intolerance brooding over the whole place which even affects Jeddah harbour. I remember being shipmate in 1913 with some eight hundred pilgrims from Aden and the southern ports of the Red Sea. As we were discharging them off Jeddah, a plump and respectable Aden merchant whom I knew by sight, but who did not know me in the guise I then wore, was gazing in rapt enthusiasm at sun-scorched Jeddah, which, against the sterile country beyond, looked like a stale bride-cake on a dust heap. "A sacred land," he crooned. "A blessed land where pigs and Christians cannot live." Incidentally he made a very good living out of Christians and was actually carrying his gear in a pigskin valise.

At the same time, it is absurd for missionaries to aver of Christians at Jeddah that "even those who die in the city are buried on an island at sea." The Christian cemetery lies to the south of the town (we had to dislodge the Turks from it with shrapnel during the fighting), and the only island is a small coral reef just big enough to support the ruins of a nondescript tenement once used for quarantine. No one could be buried there without the aid of dynamite and a cold chisel. Presumably missionary report has confused Jeddah with the smaller pilgrim-port of Yenbo, where there are an island and a sandy spit with a Sheikh's tomb and a select burial-ground for certain privileged Moslems of the holy man's family.

The worst indictment of Jeddah (and Mecca

too, for that matter) is made by the pilgrims themselves, though some of it may be exaggerated by men smarting under the extortions of pilgrim-brokers.

A pious Moslem once averred in my presence that the pilgrim-brokers of Jeddah were, in themselves, enough to bring a judgment on the place, and that trenchant opinion is not without foundation. Even to the unprejudiced eye of a travelled European they present themselves as a class of blatant bounders battening on the earnest fervour of their co-religionists and squandering the proceeds on dissipation. I have more than once been shipmate with a gang of them, and it is at sea that they cast off such restraint as the critical gaze of other Moslems might impose. As sumptuous first-class passengers they lounge about the deck in robes of tussore, rich silks and fancy waistcoats, though out of deference to their religious prejudice and Christian table-manners they usually mess by themselves. After dinner they play vociferous poker in the saloon for cut-throat stakes, evading the captain's veto by using tastefully designed little fish in translucent colours to represent heavy cash, and these they invoke from time to time "for luck." As it is usually sweltering weather, the occidental whiskey-and-soda and the aromatic *mastic* of the Levant are much in evidence, and thus three of Islam's gravest injunctions are set at naught. Their chief fault, to a broad-minded sportsman, is that they lack self-control, whatever their luck may be. I have heard an ill-starred gambler bemoaning his losses with the cries of a stricken animal, and they are still more offensive as winners.

In Mecca such open breaches of the Islamic code are not tolerated, but there are other lapses which neither Moslem nor Christian can condone. It is unfair and out of date to quote Burton's indictment of Meccan morals, nor have we any right to judge the city by its behaviour soon after its freedom from the Turkish yoke, when it may have been suffering from reaction after nervous tension; but, unless the bulk of respectable Moslem opinion is at fault, there is still much in the administration of Mecca which cries for reform. Harsh measures may have been necessary at first, but to maintain a private prison like the *Kabu* in the state it is can redound to no ruler's credit, and for prominent officials to cultivate an "alluring walk" and even practise it in the *tawâf* or circumambulation of the holy Caaba is beyond comment.

Also the mental standard of officialdom is low, since Syrians of education and training do not seem to be attracted by the Hejaz service for long, and local men of position and ability are said to have been passed over as likely to be formidable as intriguers.

It may be reasonably urged that it is difficult to improvise a Civil Service on the spur of the moment, and it is permissible to anticipate a better state of affairs now that war conditions are being superseded. At the same time it is no use blinking the fact that reform is indicated at Mecca if that sacred city is to harmonise with its high mission as the religious centre of the Islamic world, and this affects our numerous Moslem fellow-countrymen; otherwise the domestic affairs of the Hejaz are not our concern.

The Hejaz has been very much to the fore lately, and ill-informed or biassed opinion has developed a tendency to credit it with a greater part in Arabian and Syrian affairs than it has played, can play, or should be encouraged to play. Its intolerant tone has, presumably, been modified by co-operation with the civilised forces of militant Christendom, but the new kingdom has got to regenerate itself a good deal before it can cope with wider responsibilities. Emir Feisal is, no doubt, an enlightened prince, but one swallow does not make a summer, and Hejazi troops have not yet evolved enough *moral* to dominate and control a more formidable breed or be trusted with the peace and welfare of a more civilised population, especially where there are large non-Moslem communities. There has been a great deal of nonsense talked and written about their invincible fighting prowess. They accompanied the Egyptian Expeditionary Force in much the same way as the jackal is said to accompany the lion, with a reversionary interest in his kill, and their faint-hearted fumbling with the Turkish defences outside Jeddah was obvious to any observer. They are what they have been since the fiery self-sacrificing enthusiasm of early Islam died down and left them with the half-warm embers of their racial greed to become hereditary spoilers of the weak, instinctively shunning a doubtful fight. In guerilla warfare, leavened by British officers, they have shown an aptitude for taking advantage of a situation, but they cannot stand punishment and will not face the prospect of it if they can help it. Their own leaders knew that well enough when they refrained from taking Medina by assault, bombardment being out of the question, as buildings of the utmost sanctity would have been inevitably damaged or destroyed.

Prince Feisal has, in a published interview with a representative of the Press, disclaimed all imperialistic ambitions for the Hejaz, but merely demanded Arab independence in what was once the Ottoman Empire. That being assured, the new kingdom will be able to devote its energies to internal affiairs, and the excellent impression made by the Hejazi prince in Europe should be a favourable augury of the future.

The missionary question should be left to the reigning house for decision; it is not fair to hamper the Hejaz with unnecessary complications, and to allow active missionary propaganda at a pilgrim-port like Jeddah is asking for trouble, apart from the flagrant violation of religious sentiment. Imagine Catholic feeling if an enterprising Moslem mission were established at Lourdes. Tact and expediency are just as necessary in religious as in secular affairs—at least so St. Paul has taught us; but the modern missionary is too apt to regard these qualities in Christianity as insincerity and the lack of them in Islam as fanaticism.

South of the Hejaz lies that rather vague area known as Asir. For geographical purposes we may consider it as the country between two parallels of latitude drawn through the coastal towns of Lith and Loheia, with the Red Sea on the west and an ill-defined inland border merging eastward into the desert plateau of Southern Nejd. Politically, it is that territory of Western Arabia between the Hejaz and Yamen in which the Idrisi has more control than anyone since his successful revolt against the Turks a year or two before the War. In all probability its northern districts with Lith will go to the Hejaz, and the southern ones with Loheia to the Idrisi; but Western diplomacy will be well advised to leave those two rulers to settle it between themselves and the local population, especially inland, as tribal boundaries between semi-nomadic and pastoral people are not for intelligent amateurs to trifle with. Nor should the missionary be encouraged; Asir is not a suitable field for his activities, and the trouble he would probably cause is out of all proportion to the good he could possibly do. The Asiri is a frizzy-haired fanatic with a short temper and a serious disposition, addicted to sword-play and the indiscriminate use of firearms. I doubt if he would see the humour of missionary logic. As for the Idrisi himself, he is a tall, well set up man of negroid aspect (being of Moorish and Soudani descent), and has shown shrewdness as an administrator, though his operations in the War have lacked "punch." He is very orthodox, and from what I know of him I should not say that religious tolerance was his strong point. His capital is at Sabbia, in the maritime foot-hills, with a very trying climate. Asir might suit the naturalist or explorer who could adapt himself to his environment and respect local prejudice. No one has yet entered the country in either capacity, but, from what has been told me before the War by intelligent Turkish officers who campaigned there, I think that the birds and smaller mammals would repay research, while the great Dawasir valley and other geographical problems inland might be investigated with advantage under the *ægis* of local chiefs. All that is required, besides the necessary scientific knowledge and Arabic, is a certain amount of perseverance and resolution blended with a reasonable regard for other people's convictions. Most Arabian expeditions fail through lack of time spent in preliminary steps. I have tripped up in that way myself, but it was owing to the restrictions of a paternal Government, and not through lack of patience. Before I started serious exploration in the Aden hinterland I spent a year on the littoral plain getting in touch with the people and mastering the dialect. Any success I may have had up-country was due to the foundation I laid in those early days, and it was not until the Aden authorities closed their sphere of influence against exploration in general and myself in particular that my expeditions began to miss fire, as I had to land at remote places along the coast and hasten up-country before their fostering care could set the tribes on me. He who would explore Asir should take a Khedivial mail steamer from Suez to Jeddah, and there show his credentials and explain his purpose to his consul and the local authorities. The Idrisi has an agent there, and it should not be difficult to pick up an Asiri dhow returning down the coast to Gîzân, which is the port for Sabbia. He would have to stay there until he got the Idrisi's permit and an escort, without which he would be held up to a certainty. In any case, no such enterprise need be contemplated until Asiri affairs have settled down a good deal.

In Yamen proper it should be feasible to travel again within certain limits as soon as the Imam can come to an understanding with the tribal chiefs. There is not much left for the explorer or naturalist to do, unless he goes very far inland toward the great central desert, which project is not likely to be encouraged by the local authorities. There is, however, a possible field for the mineralogist and prospector east and south-east of Sanaa, which area also contains Sabæan ruins and inscriptions of interest to the archæologist.

The northern boundary of Yamen may be said nowadays to trend north-east from Loheia inland through highland country to the desert borders of Nejran (once a Christian diocese). Its eastern border is very vague, but may be said to coincide approximately with the 45th parallel of longitude. Southward the limit has been clearly defined by the Anglo-Turkish Boundary Commission of 1902–5 inland from the Bana valley, about a hundred map-miles north of Aden, to the straits of Bab-el-Mandeb.

Within these limits the two great divisions of Islam are represented in force—the orthodox *Sunnis* on the littoral plain and far inland along the upland deserts, while the highlanders among the lofty fertile ranges separating these two areas and forming the backbone of the country follow the *Shiah* schism, being Zeidis, which of all the schismatic sects approaches most nearly to orthodox Islam and regards Mecca as its pilgrim-centre. The feeling between these two religious divisions may be compared with that existing between Anglicans and Catholics. They will occasionally use each other's places of worship—more especially the upper or governing classes—and seldom come to open loggerheads; when they do, it is usually about politics, and not religion. At the same time, if you, as a Christian traveller among both parties, want a scathing opinion of a Zeidi, you will get it from an orthodox lowlander, and the men of the mountains reciprocate with point and weight, for the balance of religious culture and position is with them among the big hill-centres; including Sanaa, the political capital where the Imam holds, or should hold, his court as hereditary ruler spiritual and temporal. This ecclesiastical potentate has backed the Turk in a non-committal but flamboyant manner during the War up to the turning of the tide against them, when he sat on the fence until his Turkish subsidy ceased. He now looks to Western diplomacy in general and the British Government in particular not only to continue but to enhance this subsidy, in order that he may really govern in Yamen. His attitude throughout is natural and, indeed, justifiable in the interests of himself and his dynasty; at least occidental politicians cannot cavil at his motives; but what they ought to ascertain is how far he can fill the bill as a ruler in Yamen and the extent to which he should be backed. Without a considerable subsidy his administrative powers (not hitherto very marked) will not carry far even in the highlands.

Missionaries were allowed to enter Yamen before the War, but did not establish themselves, even on the coast. Some of them went up-country and stayed there some time without being molested. The average Yameni is not fanatical by temperament; there is more bigotry among the urban Jew colonies than in the whole Moslem countryside.

In the Aden protectorate there has been long established the Falconer Medical Mission, which, though actually at Sheikh Othman, just inside the British border, has done splendid work among natives of the hinterland, who visit it from all parts. Its relations with the Arabs have always been excellent, though the local ruffians looted the Mission when the Turks held Sheikh Othman temporarily.

The province of Hadhramaut, politically, includes not only the vast valley of that name with its tributaries, but the whole of the western part of Southern Arabia outside the Aden protectorate from the Yamen border to the confines of Oman near longitude 55. Mokalla is the capital and principal port. Missionaries have been well received there by the enlightened ruler—a member of the Kaaiti house with the local title of Jemadar, inherited from an ancestor who soldiered in the Arab bodyguard of a former Nizam at Haiderabad. The interior is not suited to missionary enterprise.

Muscat, the capital of Oman, has already been occupied by missionaries. The Sultan (at whose court there is a British Resident) is well-disposed, but has lost most of his influence inland.

Further up the Persian Gulf missionaries have long been established on the islands of Bahrein, which are under British protection.

Continuing our journey eastward, we can dismiss the Shiahs of Persia as outside our pan-Islamic calculations, for their pilgrim-centre is at Kerbela, some twenty odd miles west of the Euphrates and the site of ancient Babylon. This centre has been visited by missionaries.

Afghanistan and Beluchistan both bar missionaries, but there are C.M.S. frontier posts from Quetta, in British Beluchistan, to Peshawar, near the Afghan border. They do good hospital work, otherwise their evangelising activities over the border are confined to native colporteurs and the circulation of vernacular Scriptures. There is a fierce and barbarous Turcoman spirit in both countries which their respective rulers (the Khan of Kelat and the Emir at Cabul) do their best to keep within bounds, aided by British Residents. Missionaries seem to think this spirit can be exorcised by their entrance into the arena. You might as well throw squibs into a cage full of tigers.

On entering India (that vast hunting-ground of many sects and creeds), Moslem and missionary are almost swamped in the flood of Hinduism. There is no restriction on the activities of either within the four corners of the King-Emperor's peace, and there is very little antagonism between the two in so big a field, where both are doing good work. Although the Moslems outnumber the Christians by seven to one, the honours of war go to the missionaries. Their highly-organised medical and educational missions do excellent work—the Zenana Mission is, in itself, a justification of Christian mission work in India to any humanitarian with some knowledge of *zenana* conditions. The Moslems, on the other hand, in spite of their high standard of education, in India show a tendency among their less educated classes toward the caste prejudices of Hinduism, which are dead against the teaching of Islam and a handicap to any social organisation.

Few people realise what a huge proposition the Indian Empire is to solve in its entirety, with its population of 315 millions, of whom over 90 per cent. are illiterate. Of the more or less educated residuum, not quite 90 per cent. are Brahmins having little in common with the huge uneducated bulk of the population, which is chiefly agricultural and, by its patient toil, supplies most of the wealth of India. Yet it is the cultured but unproductive Brahmin (organised by a brainy old lady) who wants to control the native affairs of India—and probably will.

In Farther India the Brahmin is at a discount and the Buddhist is to the fore, while Moslem and missionary are far too busy among the heathen to bother about each other; as also in Malay, where there is field enough and to spare for both of them.

The only other debatable field in Asia is that vast area which we call China, comprising China proper, Manchuria, Mongolia, Tibet and Eastern Turkestan. Moslem and missionary can hardly be said to meet face to face, as missionary enterprise is chiefly in China itself, where the great waterways have been of much assistance to Christian activities, while Moslem efforts are concentrated on Chinese Turkestan. Here there are two Christian missions, at Yarkand and Kashgar, under the protection (as elsewhere in China) of the Chinese Government. Moslem propaganda is spread by traders and others working from centres of Islamic learning outside Chinese territory, such as Bokhara and Samarkand in Russian Turkestan, and Cabul, the Afghan capital. In addition, there is a wave of Chinese secular culture lapping in from the East, and missionaries ask that existing missions be reinforced with funds to take a more effective part in this battle for souls (as they express it). They complain bitterly that the upper classes *will* send their sons away to places like Bokhara to be educated, and that they come back Moslems. They also call for ample funds to attack Islam on its own ground in Russian Turkestan, as it is permeating Christian Russia. This missionary point of view is natural enough; how far it is justifiable is for the contributing public to decide. To the ordinary mind Christian villages which can become Moslem by the leavening influence of a few inhabitants who have been to work in Moslem centres convey one of two impressions, or both: either Christianity is not adapted to their requirements so much as Islam, or they are too weak-kneed to be a credit to any faith, and the one with the most virile methods may take them and make men of them if it can. Moslem and missionary activities in Chinese Asia remind one of cheese-mites gnawing away on opposite sides of a Double Gloucester. They are very active, and if they keep at it may get through some day; but meanwhile the cheese seems much the same as ever, apart from its own internal changes which the mites cannot control or affect.

We will now turn to Africa, the main theatre of war between Moslem and missionary, who battle with each other for pagan souls and each other's proselytes.

We will first visit Morocco, the most westerly of

Moslem countries. Here there is not much missionary activity, either Protestant or Catholic, but the French have been doing some excellent secular work there, and under their tutelage the country is developing on lines of moderate progress.

There is little antipathy shown to missionaries here, at any rate on the coast, and medical missionaries have been welcomed inland. Education does not flourish, but the country might be described by an unbiassed observer as enlightened at least as far south as a line joining Mogador and Morocco City (Marrakesh). In this northern area you will find an industrious agricultural population of small farmers scattered about the countryside, which consists of wide, open tracts of arable land under millet, maize, and other cereals, dotted here and there with groves of olive and orange and interspersed with large forests of *argan* and other small trees. Desert country encroaches more and more toward the south, and in spite of several large streams draining into the Atlantic from the snowcapped Atlas range, the country becomes very wild and sterile the farther south you go from Mogador until it merges in the Sahara, across which lies the great, bone-whitened highway that leads to Timbuctoo.

Whatever the indigenous Berber of the Atlas

may be, the northern Moor has never been a mere barbarian, and Spain owes much to his culture and industry. He certainly used to have a bizarre conception of international amenities, and got himself very much disliked in the Mediterranean and even northern waters in consequence. That phase, however, has long since passed; the last corsair has rotted at its moorings in Sallee harbour, and I am told that to put a wealthy Jew in a thing like a giant trouser-press and extort money under pressure is considered now an anachronism.

When I first knew the country, a quarter of a century ago, it was just emerging from a revolutionary war, and local relations with foreigners or even neighbours were capricious. They murdered a German bagman up the coast in an *argan* forest, and the "Gefion" landed a flag-flaunting armed party to impress Mogador, which dropped water-pitchers on them from upper windows and wondered what on earth the fuss was about.

On the other hand, I was well received by one of the revolted tribes, which had chased its lawful Kaid into Mogador until checked by old scrap-iron and bits of bottle-glass from the ancient cannon mounted over the northern gate of the town.

I was treated with far more hospitality than my absurd and rather rash enterprise deserved. Imagine a callow youth just out of his teens dropping in haphazard on a rebel tribe accompanied by a mission-taught Moor and a large liver-coloured pointer who had far more sense than his master. My tame Moor was an excellent fellow, who, beside keeping my tent tidy and cooking, helped me to grapple with the derived forms of the Arabic verb and the subtleties of Moorish etiquette. I learnt to drink green tea, syrup-sweet and flavoured with mint, out of ornate little tumblers of a size and shape usually associated with champagne, and, after assiduous practice, I could tackle a dish of boiled millet, meat, and olives with the fingers of my right hand without mishap.

Beyond occasional brushes with adjacent sections of the neighbouring tribe which had declared for the Fez central Government, I had very little trouble, except that a peaceful boar-hunt would occasionally degenerate into an intertribal skirmish if I and my party got too near the loyalist border. As all concerned had, thanks to Western enterprise, discarded their picturesque flint-locks in favour of Winchester or Marlin repeaters, the proceedings required wary handling if we were to extricate ourselves successfully, but my long-range sporting Martini usually gave me the weather-gauge.

I dressed as a Moor, and looked the part, but made no attempt to pass for anything but a Christian, nor did any unpopularity attach thereto; I was merely expected—as a natural corollary—to have a little medical knowledge (and it *was* a little).

I found the attitude of Moors generally towards Christians curiously inconsistent. In the towns there was a certain amount of formal fanaticism which found vent in donkey-drivers addressing their beasts as "*Nasara*" to the accompaniment of whacks and yells, but public behaviour was tolerant enough, and the attitude of Moorish officialdom was almost courtly.

Jews had rather a bad time, if local subjects, as their black slippers and furtive bearing outside their own quarter made them a mark for naughty little boys, who flung their canary-coloured slippers at them with curses and imprecations deserving a more direct and personal application of their footgear. Most of the wealthier Jews had acquired European or American protection, and were safe enough. They lived in the Frankish quarter and dressed in ultra-European style. They made rather a depressing spectacle on Saturdays, when, garbed in black broadcloth, with bowler hats, they drifted through the sunlit streets on their Sabbath constitutional from one town gate to the next and back. They were keen trade competitors, and gained or lost fortunes by gambling in the almond export-market or catching a grain-famine at the psychological moment. One of them had retired to a leisured affluence on the proceeds that a big cargo of almonds had yielded him at a startling turn in the market. He was a hospitable soul who met me once entering the landward gate in a travel-stained burnoose and insisted on dragging me into his gorgeously-carpeted house to drink *aquardiente* and look at his "curios." These consisted chiefly of modern firearms, some of first-class London make, which hung on his walls as ornaments, having been bought haphazard without ammunition or sporting intent. I nearly had a fit when he showed me a double .577 Express hopelessly rusted by the damp sea-air and offered to lend it me if I could find "shots" for it. The reverse of the shield was illustrated by another acquaintance of mine who had made a large fortune by importing Russian wheat to Morocco in famine time and had lost it in a short but striking career in England, during which he was said to have entertained Royalty, astonished the racing world and married a well-known actress in light comedy. He, too, was of hospitable intent, but had generally left his purse at home when the reckoning came. On the other hand, he always carried the "stub" of the cheque-book which had seen him to the apogee of his meteoric career, and a glance at its counterfoils (by his express invitation) was well worth the price of a drink or two.

The local Islamic attitude toward Moorish Jews was one of contemptuous tolerance. They could certainly travel, in native dress, where no Christian could. Once, in the *patio* or go-down of a European merchant, I met a greasy, unkempt Jew in a tattered gaberdine watching my commercial friend as he weighed what I took to be a double handful of crude brass curtain rings such as traders used to sell by the gross along the West African coast. They were solid gold and represented the venture of a Jewish syndicate which had collected it in pinches of gold-dust from the river beds of southern Soos and hit on this form of transport. A troop of horse could never have brought it, as gold, a day's journey through the lawless tribes of the south, but that tatterdemalion Jew had done it at the price of a few contemptuous buffets. He had, indeed, offered one truculent gang of highwaymen a few of the tawdry-looking rings to let him pass, but they had waved such obvious trash aside in their eager search for actual cash, which they had taken to the last *rial.*

The only other occasion on which I have known a Moor to be hoisted with the petard of his own contemptuous fanaticism was an experience of my own.

I was moving quietly through a belt of timber just before dawn in the hopes of getting a shot at a boar who was in the habit of feeding till daybreak among some barley that grew near a caravan route. Before the light was quite strong enough to shoot by I was more than a little annoyed and astonished to hear cocks crowing all over the place; presuming an early caravan with poultry for market, I pushed on to the track, meaning to pass the time of day and ask if they had glimpsed my quarry or heard him. I almost ran into a town-bred Moor who was trying to round up some scattered poultry in the gloom and cursing volubly. He explained that he was riding his donkey along the track perched between two light reed cages containing fowls when the donkey baulked as a boar snorted in the thickets just off the road. He whacked the donkey and cursed the boar as a pig and a Christian. Thereupon came a rush like cavalry, the donkey was knocked from under him and he was lying amid the wreckage of his flimsy crates with his poultry scattered abroad. The boar, already angry and suspicious, as anyone but a townsman would have known by the noise he made, had charged like a thunderbolt at the sound of a human voice so close to him and galloped off with all the honours of war.

The donkey was badly hurt and the man only escaped because he was sitting high and just above the point of impact. I helped him secure his poultry and started back to my village to send him another donkey. He thanked me in brotherly style as one Moor to another. "I'm a Christian myself," I remarked at parting, and added in my best beginner's Arabic as I turned to go, "It is incumbent on me to assist you after the aggression of my co-religionist."

This conventional attitude of arrogance toward Christendom is perhaps traceable to Moorish predominance in the Middle Ages and the importation of Christian slaves by the pirates of the Barbary coast. In any case, it has been much toned down of late years owing to contact with capable and well-intentioned Franks as administrators and technical experts.

Morocco should never become a forcing-bed of religious or racial antipathy, and will not so long as France continues to develop the country by methods which the natives can assimilate, and is not lured into over-exploitation of her mineral resources or unwarrantable interference with her spiritual affairs.

A perfectly justifiable missionary policy would be the inauguration of industrial schools on the coast and at one or two big inland centres, also medical missions (with consent of the local authorities) wherever feasible. Moorish craftsmanship is worth stimulating, and doctors are welcomed for their science. Both schemes would redound to the credit of Christendom and be in accordance with the best traditions of the Early Church.

In the other Barbary states (Algeria, Tunis and Tripoli) a few Catholic missions have been established, and the North African Protestant Mission has an advanced post at Kairwan in Tunis. Here many routes converge, for Kairwan is a great centre of pilgrimage and taps the religious thought of all the Saharan tribes. Under such conditions, Islam gets ahead every time, as every caravan traveller is a potential missionary, while Christian missions are anchored to the spot or have to rely on native colporteurs, who labour under the initial disadvantage of being proselytes and seldom have the combination of tact and staunchness which evangelists require.

It is in Egypt that we first find Moslem and missionary at close grips arrayed against each other. Cairo is a perfect cockpit of creeds. Christianity is represented by Catholics, Copts, Orthodox Greeks and Protestants, these last being subdivided into Anglicans, Presbyterians, Wesleyans and American Presbyterians and Congregationalists. The main body of Islam—some of my more fervent missionary friends allude to it as "the hosts of Midian"—presents a fairly solid front of orthodoxy, the bulk being Hanifis, Shafeis, Maliki or Hanbalis (chiefly the two former); but the irregular forces of Shiah are well represented among non-indigenous Moslems from Yamen, Persia and India, while scattered groups of Wahabi ascetics, Sufi mystics and esoterics of Bahaism skirmish on debatable ground between the opposing lines, where range such free-lance companies as Theosophists, Christian Scientists, Salvationists, etc., all with local headquarters in Cairo and propaganda of their own.

It must not be supposed that all this warlike metaphor indicates actual strife or even severe friction, any more than "the hosts of Midian" represents the attitude of missionaries to Moslems here. On the contrary, relations are for the most part excellent, and the prevailing animosity is political, not religious, being directed against us British much as normal schoolboys dislike their form-master until they get a harsher one.

The Catholic Church confines most of her energies to teaching her own people, who are very numerous and well looked after; she does not do much alien mission work in this part of the world. The most formidable band of gladiators in the Christian ranks is the American Protestant Mission, and next to them the Anglican C.M.S. (chiefly distinguished in Egypt for its medical work, which is excellent and has an extraordinarily wide range). The Americans are great on education and have done more for the English language in Cairo than any Government institution. I use the term "gladiators" advisedly, for their most trenchant work is done on their own side—they concentrate their chief efforts on the Copts, and make a fairly good bag of proselytes from them, apart from the great number to whom they teach sound ideals of duty as well as English and the three "R's." One of their leading missionaries has left it on record that no one stands more in need of salvation than the Copts, and as there is a Coptic Reform Society the Copts must think there is room for improvement too.

It has been found in practice that to convert

a *bonâ-fide* Moslem involves segregating him, and that means finding him a living in a new environment, otherwise he is almost bound to "revert" under local pressure. Apart from the strain on mission resources which such procedure would cause if extensively followed, most missionaries rightly condemn such a system as encouraging conversion for material motives. Therefore they adopt a policy of "peaceful penetration" against Islam, encouraging young men to come to them unostentatiously (I call them the Nicodemus-squad) in order to discuss religious questions, which is usually done in a temperate and intelligent manner on both sides. Even if they get no "forrader," it tends to toleration and a better knowledge of each other's language and ideals. A good deal of teaching is done too with no expectation of making proselytes, and solid friendships are formed. I have myself known a convalescing lady missionary of the C.M.S. to receive repeated calls of friendly inquiry from former pupils; when I first saw two veiled young girls swing past with a palpably British terrier and the crisp, vigorous step of occidental emancipation, it puzzled my ethnological faculties until I was told the object of their visit.

All this is to the good, and it would be very

good indeed if they let well alone. Unfortunately, there is another cogent factor in the mission field, and that is the sinews of war in hard cash. Most people, even those who support missions to Moslem countries, are human enough to like a fight put up for their money. It is not enough for them that a great deal of quiet, patient work is being done by missionaries among Moslems in the name of Christianity and the service of mankind. They want to hear about storming citadels of sin and campaigning against the devil in the dark places of the earth; especially is this so in America, where Moslem prejudice does not have to be considered and religious organisation, like most other concerns, is on a big scale.

As a natural consequence, missionaries have to play up to this combatant instinct, and so we read in their books and reports remarks calculated to engender religious intolerance on both sides, and which do not conform with the shrewd and kindly work in the field of those devoted and often scholarly men. I shall have occasion to allude to some of these statements as we proceed, so think it only fair to mention their justification here.

Cairo is described as a "strategic centre" in mission parlance, and so it is, being situated on a great waterway with rail connection far south into the heart of Africa and converging caravan routes from every quarter. Along these arteries of traffic many tons of tracts and propaganda are hurled annually by train, felucca and colporteur. Those who cannot read accept such matter gladly to wrap things up in and to show to their literate friends, who read what resembles a bit of the Koran and find it carries a sting in its tail, like a scorpion, aimed at Islam. A great deal of this literature consists of the Psalms of David, the Talmud or the Gospel, all reverenced by Moslems if dished up without trimmings. Not wishing to impose on that hard-worked word "camouflage," I would merely ask, as a naturalist, if such protective mimicry is worth the irritation it causes. In any case, the system reminds me of an old Highlander's opening comment on a sword dance by a rock scorpion in a Tangier saloon. "There is a sairtain elegance aboot yourr grace-steps, but *get in between the swords.*"

No vicarious efforts by propaganda will ever take the place of personal precept and example. In hunting proselytes among the followers of Islam it is not advisable to rely too much on the Scriptures, as Moslems doubt the authenticity of our version and point to our own divergent copies in proof thereof. Nor is it any use asking them to believe as an act of faith; if they did they would need no proselytising: an appeal must be made to their reason, and there is no better appeal than the life, works, and conduct of one who professes and practises Christianity. Even if he makes no single convert he has leavened the population around him with the dignity and prestige of his creed which has produced such a type. Unfortunately such results cannot be scheduled in mission reports, though they are real enough and well worth living for, whether a man be a missionary or not; only they cannot be produced by brilliant wide-sweeping feats of organisation and enterprise, but by persevering, consistent lives, which are not easy or spectacular.

Egypt should be a great field of religious warfare by personal influence, as Christians and Moslems live side by side in daily contact and reasonable accord, yet few of us take advantage of the fact to uphold the prestige of our creed or even of our race. We Europeans are busy with our multifarious interests and duties, while Egyptian Moslems are either entangled in the web of their environment, as are the *fellahin*, or eager snatchers at the gifts of civilisation, as are the more or less cultured effendis, or mere hair-splitters in futile religious controversy, as are too many of the *ulema* or sages at the great collegiate mosque of al-Azhar. In each case, spiritual matters are apt to get crowded out. The fault lies chiefly with our cosmopolitan ingredients, which engender feverish living, if not actual vice, and the over-strained effort on the one side to impart and on the other side to assimilate a Western system of education which has induced intellectual dyspepsia. So we hear of students mugging parrot-like to pass half-yearly examinations, in the hopes of getting Government appointments for which there are far too many applicants; these young men besiege the Press with complaints of unfair treatment if they fail, or even go to the length of attempting suicide with carbolic acid (fortunately with sufficient caution to ensure it usually being but an attempt); this latter petulant protest at the temporary thwarting of their material hopes is dead against all the teaching and tradition of Islam, but it has become so frequent that a leading educational authority suggests that no student who attempts suicide shall be allowed to sit again for a Government examination. Among their seniors up at al-Azhar are men of real learning and remarkably persevering scholarship (their theological course makes the average brain reel to contemplate), but some sheikh started a controversy as to whether Adam was a prophet or not, which fell among those sages with the disrupting force of a grenade, causing much litigation in the Islamic courts and culminating in the divorce of the originator by his wife for *kufr*, or heresy as ordained by Moslem law. Beneath these troubled waters the *fellah's* life flows placidly, bounded on the one hand by his crops and on the other by the market; his spiritual stimulus being supplied by an occasional religious fair or a visit to the shrine of some local saint. He toils as patiently as his water-wheel buffalo, and on that toil depends the wealth of Egypt which supports saints and sinners, schools and shops, with all our European schemes and enterprises thrown in.

As for us British, if our object is to enhance the prestige of our race or creed, we fall very short of achievement. We have not even that reputation for integrity which usually attaches to us in other parts of the Moslem world. This may be partly due to our anomalous position in the country, which was thrust upon us, but the pleasure-seeking tourist of pre-War days has a lot to answer for. Some of them seemed to think that so far from home their conduct was of no account (at least, that is the only charitable explanation), and British personal prestige suffered in consequence. Anglo-Egyptian officials, especially the subordinate grades, which come into more direct contact with the people, tried to counteract this by increased dignity of demeanour, but the natives now knew them *en déshabillé*, or thought they did, and declined to keep them on their pedestals. The result is, familiarity without intimacy and detachment without dignity, while the pre-War official habit of going Home every year for some months has prevented even subordinates from studying their district or department consecutively.

Hence it is that a widespread Nationalits movement gathered force and perfected its plans for a detailed campaign which blended peaceful demonstration with sabotage, murder and violence, and took the Anglo-Egyptian Government completely by surprise, paralysing communications and intimidating the general public until the weight of Imperial troops, luckily still quartered in the country, was allowed to make itself felt and restored order.

This is not the time or the place to discuss these affairs, which are still *sub judice*, but one salient feature of the movement is pertinent to our subject, and that is the marked *rapprochement* between Moslems and Copts, who fraternised in each other's mosques and churches, carried flags bearing the device of Cross and Crescent and used American mission buildings to further their new-found brotherhood. These relations were somewhat marred by the wholesale devastation of Coptic property up-country, but the Copts took it very well and paraded the streets with their Moslem friends, if they could not hide away from them. The local Jew came in too, and the climax of this religious *entente* was reached when an Egyptian Jewess preached in the mosque of al-Azhar on the ancient relations between Jews and Arabs.

But we must not merely consider Egypt as a sort of religious and racial clearing house; it is also the main gate of Africa.

Southward, up the Nile valley and across grim deserts, lies Khartoum, the capital of the Anglo-Egyptian Sudan, only four days from Cairo by rail. This is a very tempting theatre for missionary enterprise, which is, however, held in check by the authorities, who decline to have their Sudan spiritually exploited and materially disturbed by futile efforts to evangelise the country. Missionaries say that this part of the Sudan, as well as Egypt, was once Christian; that discrimination is being shown in favour of Islam even to the extent of making pagans become Moslem on joining the Egyptian Army; that Gordon College is being run on non-Christian lines and that Islam is getting ahead of them in the race to convert pagans in this part of the world.

The case against them is that the fact of these regions being once Christian and now Moslem shows, if anything, that the latter religion is more suited to local requirements and conditions; Islam is naturally favoured in a Moslem country, though many Christian missions have been given facilities too, and have mostly failed owing to climatic conditions: the Egyptian Army is Moslem and under a Moslem Government; the conversion of pagan recruits to Islam is encouraged for the sake of discipline and soldierly conduct; missionaries themselves admit that even in civil life a Christian convert from Islam must be segregated or he will lapse under surrounding pressure—perhaps they will explain how that is to be done in a barrack-room or native infantry lines, or would they prefer such recruits to remain pagan? Presumably they would, as one of their complaints is that "it is a thousand times harder to convert a Moslem to Christianity than a pagan." Comment is superfluous; nothing could portray their attitude more clearly. As for Islam getting ahead of them in the race for pagan souls, it is so and will be so always among the black races unless Christian missions are bolstered up by all the resources of local

M 2

authority; the reason is that Islam offers equal privileges and no colour-line, imposes easy spiritual obligations and is propagated fervently by its followers without the encumbrance of an organised priesthood. Just as commercial travellers consider a district neglected where a rival firm has got ahead of them, so missionaries are piqued at conditions in the Sudan; but even that does not excuse such statements as that women in the Sudan are free and not badly treated as pagans, but slaves and oppressed under Islam. Every student of the Islamic code knows that the status of women has been enormously improved thereby as compared with any pagan system. Missionaries must know this, for they are much better educated about Islam than they were a quarter of a century ago, yet they do not scruple to raise the partisan cry of a debased womanhood under Islam wherever local conditions involve domestic hardship. Such tactics are unworthy of them; an intellectual Moslem does not reproach Christianity because he has visited districts in the poorer quarters of our big towns and seen women lead lives of drudgery or being sometimes knocked about by their husbands.

Outside the Sudan and Nigeria we must keep to the eastern side of Africa in order to maintain touch with Islam. The negroid people of Italian Erythrea are Moslems, as are also the Somalis; but their racial cousins, the Abyssinians, are Christians of the Ethiopian Church, with the Negus as their temporal and spiritual ruler, who claims descent from King Solomon and the Queen of Sheba.

Abyssinia has been Christian ever since the fourth century, but the missionaries are not happy about the country at all. Here nothing impedes the entrance of the missionary as an individual, but the people will not have him as an evangelist at any price. The "fanatical and debased" priests of the Abyssinian Church and the drastic punishments inflicted by the local authorities on those suspected of favouring other forms of Christianity are described as grave hindrances. There is a large population of "black Jews," who will have no dealings with Christianity in any form. Meanwhile Islam gains ground steadily, especially in the south along the trade routes. A German missionary, writing from Strasburg in 1910, describes the situation as alarming, because "whole tribes of Abyssinians who still bear Christian names have become Muhammedans in the last twenty years." There is one Protestant mission up at Addis Abeba, but it confines its attentions to the semi-pagan

Gallas, having given up Christian Abyssinia as a bad job.

Somaliland is a poor field for missionary enterprise, owing to the sparse, semi-nomadic population and the difficulties of getting about. In the French sphere there is connection by rail between Jibuti on the coast and Dera Dowa near the Abyssinian border; travelling musicians of the *café chantant* type used to use it a good deal before the War, but there was not much doing in the missionary line. Italian Somaliland, east of the British sphere to Cape Guardafui, is left to look after itself, except for the occasional visit of an Italian man-of-war; but south of that great headland there are Italian settlements.

In British Somaliland missionary enterprise has hitherto been Catholic, and even that ceased some years before the War when the authorities had to tell the mission that it must leave, as they could no longer protect it from the Mullah's people. It was a pity, as the mission was doing good work and was much respected in the country. There was a Brotherhood which taught and doctored, and a teaching Sisterhood. They were Franciscans and had their local headquarters and a tastefully designed little chapel in the native town of Berbera, but the Brothers had also an agricultural settlement up-country, where they tilled the soil and did their best to teach the natives to do so too. The Somali is much easier to convert than the Arab, as his versatile and superficial temperament induces him to imitate, if not to assimilate, alien forms and ceremonies from the correct procedure at the "Angelus" to the singing, with appropriate gestures, of "a bicycle made for two." Unfortunately, it is almost impossible to teach him to think, or to do a day's honest work; he will pull a punkah while you are awake to keep him at it, or row a boat if allowed to sing, and sometimes he will fish if hungry and quite near the sea; but agriculture involves the hard work of digging, and that is too much for him. The object of the mission was to give Somali boys and girls the rudiments of Catholic Christianity and habits of industry. The boys were well grounded in English and the three "R's" in their simplest form, while the girls were taught chiefly sewing and cooking. The idea was for boys and girls to marry each other in the fulness of time and beget Christian children, but, as one of the good Fathers used regretfully to say, it did not work out in practice. The boys learnt enough to become interpreters or obtain small clerkships in the post and telegraph offices of Aden and adjacent ports, whereupon they felt marriage with a "black woman" to be derogatory, and looked higher, to the less swarthy charms of some half-caste maiden met at Mass (for they usually remained Catholic, at least in outward form). The girls, on the other hand, with all their domestic training, were much sought after by local chiefs, who were prepared to give them a good allowance in beads, bangles and cloth, plenty of food and a fairly easy life. In such surroundings they naturally readopted Islam.

Somaliland is not as barren as most people suppose. Of course the littoral plain is comparatively sterile, as is the case on the Arabian side, owing to the scanty rainfall, and the maritime scarp of the hills that back it is not much better, but the country improves as you go inland; there is good grazing on the intra-montane plateau, and the watersheds of such massifs as Wagr, Sheikh and Golis (7,000 ft. or so) are thickly wooded, chiefly with the gigantic cactus tree, which averages forty feet; timber trees are scarce, being mostly tall *Coniferæ* in sheltered glens at the higher altitudes. Inland of these ranges the ground slopes gradually toward the almost waterless Haud—a vast plateau sparsely covered with tall mimosa bush or actual trees attaining some thirty feet in height and striking deep to subterranean moisture, which keeps them remarkably fresh and green. Giraffe feed eagerly on the tender upper foliage and herds of camel graze there too, going six months without water, for there is no known supply locally except in the occasional mud-pans or *ballis* after a rainburst, which may happen once a year. These camels are kept for meat and milk only, and are no use for transport, as they are too "soft" to carry a sack of flour. They are rounded up and brought in to wells twice a year, where they water for a week or so. Herdsmen moving with them live on their milk, which is most sustaining. They must be watered after a maximum interval of half a year, or they get "poor" and will not put on flesh. Needless to say, no transport camel could be treated like that. A caravan camel can go five days without water, but that is about his limit while working, and he should be allowed to rest and graze for some days afterwards if he is to regain working condition. The giraffe, as also antelope of various kinds, can support life without water at all, though they trek greedily to the *ballis* after rain. Here lion lie in wait for them occasionally, and it is a frequent subject of discussion among naturalists and sportsmen how such heavy, thirsty animals can subsist in the Haud. The most probable supposition is that they only enter this region with the rains and trek from one *balli* to another. I have met a lioness a long way out of lion country presumably trekking from one water-hole to the next. What is still more remarkable is that heavy game sometimes will do so too. Heavy firing was once heard far south of Burao, and a mounted force pushed out thinking it was the Mullah's people going for our "friendlies" out grazing. A rhinoceros on trek for water and nearly mad with thirst had winded the waterskins in a Somali grazing camp and charged through the zareba to get at them. He was mobbed to death by the herdsmen with the rifles which a benevolent Government had given them for protection against the dervishes.

To do them justice, the Somalis fear their fauna very little and have more than once, when in attendance on a European sportsman, driven off a lion with spears and a resolute front after the white man had failed to stop the beast with both barrels.

Even a woman will face a leopard with a torch of dry grass to contest the ownership of a fat-tailed sheep which he has tried to filch from the zareba by night, fearing his snarling menace far less than the wrath of her lord and master if the marauder secures his prey.

As for the Midgan, that born hunter and nomadic outcast whom other Somalis look down upon, but who has more woodcraft in his touzled head than any of them, he will deliberately hunt the king of beasts, using some decrepit and almost valueless camel as a stalking-horse. He is armed with a bow having about as much apparent "give" in it as the bottom joint of a fishing rod, yet able to propel with surprising force a stumpy arrow cunningly poisoned with a wizard brew of viper venom and the root of the tall box tree. His procedure is to drive his camel slowly grazing toward some island of bush in which he has marked down a lion, he himself being perched a-straddle behind the hump and directing the animal's movements with kicks from one or other of his bare heels. From his lofty observation point he at once spots the crouching approach of the lion and slips off over the camel's rump to cover, whence he speeds one of his venomous little shafts at close range. The outraged monarch attacks the camel and the hunter keeps well aloof from the subsequent confusion until the poison works and the lion is seized with muscular convulsions, like those of tetanus, when he may safely approach to gloat over his quarry. What is really remarkable is that the camel is not invariably killed. I once met a Midgan on trek who showed me the unmistakable claw-marks of a lion on his camel's neck and shoulders and said he had used the animal on three such occasions;

compared with these desperate encounters the exploits of our white shikaris armed with powerful modern rifles are insignificant.

One beast of prey, however, is feared and hated by every Somali man, woman or child—hunter, shepherd or townsman—and that is the great, spotted hyæna which slinks up by night to snap at face or breast of sleeping folk and bolts into the gloom at the agonised shriek of his mangled victim. The brute is cowardly enough to refuse encounter with an able-bodied man awake and on the alert unless rendered desperate by hunger, but his jaws are as strong as a lion's, and one snapping bite does the mischief. I once helped the P.M.O. at Berbera to tend some half-dozen poor wretches who had been frightfully mauled during the night on the outskirts of the town itself and probably by the same hyæna. The hot weather had induced many folk to sleep outside their stifling huts and they *will* not take the trouble to collect and build up a few thorny bushes to keep the brutes off.

The Somali is about as incapable of hard work as his "fat" camel, and the only time he may be seen digging is among the convict gangs who till, or used to till, the Government garden out at Dubar on the inland edge of the littoral plain, where the Berbera water supply bubbles out hot from under the low maritime hills and trickles through ten miles of surface pipe-line to supply the "Fort," which is supposed to protect the British cantonment straggling some distance outside Berbera town. He feels such work dreadfully, not only as an injury to his self-respect (and he has all the puerile pride of the negroid races), but as an irksome tax on his physical powers, which are quite unaccustomed to sustained and strenuous exertion. On the other hand, he will make long journeys on short commons and keep well and happy if allowed to punctuate his hardships at long intervals with debauches on meat and milk and fat. He excuses himself from tilling the ground on the plea that others might harvest the fruit of his labours, as there is no individual land-tenure or any definite divisions of land indicating ownership, but only tribal grazing rights over ill-defined areas and the parcel of land enclosed by his zareba fence, of which he is but the tenant, as it is free to anybody as soon as he leaves it to trek to other pastures. Therefore, vegetables are unattainable by him, and his cereals (rice, millet and coarse flour) reach him by sea and caravan or he does without. He appears immune from scurvy and is seldom sick or sorry unless he over-eats himself. He loves *ghi* (or clarified butter) and animal fat, which he swallows in large gulps when he can get it, also rubbing it in his frizzy hair and using it to sleek his black, spindly shanks and smear his spear-blades—on shikar he will "gorm" it all over your spare gun if you do not watch him. His favourite beverage is strong tea with lots of sugar in it (when procurable) otherwise he will not touch it, and he will drink water which a thirsty camel would sniff at suspiciously before imbibing. He dresses in a white sheet worn toga-wise and not without a certain dignity, and his head is usually bare except in towns or the partially civilised *entourage* of a white man, where he will wear anything on his head from a tarboosh to a topi as a mark of distinction, but seems to avoid a turban, which he has not the knack of tying properly.

To meet him and his family on trek is to glimpse an epitome of his life. First comes the able-bodied though elderly sire carrying a few light throwing-spears and a knobkerry or a gim-crack stabbing-spear, and close behind him are the adult males of his house similarly armed or with a rifle or two supplied by a benevolent Government for protection against the Mullah, to whom these children of nature frequently offer them for sale at very reasonable prices. After these come the women-folk in order of precedence, carrying loads in inverse ratio thereto. The young, favourite wife walks first, carrying her latest addition to the family in a cotton shawl at her hip; she is followed by other wives of less social standing, carrying household utensils, with the smaller children at foot, and at the tail of the procession stagger the old crones under heavy burdens of pots, pans, pitchers and unsavoury goat-hair rugs. A camel or two bring up the rear with the conglomeration of sticks and hides and matting which makes the home and looks like an untidy bird's nest. On the flanks and in the rear skirmish the elder children, girls and boys, with flocks and herds which graze as they go. The big piebald sheep with their black heads and indecently fat tails are not allowed to range far afield, where lynx or leopard might stalk them under covert, as they are valuable, succulent and very foolish. They carry no wool—their coat feels just like a fox-terrier's—but they have more meat on them than three average goats, and the huge pendulous flap of fat which does duty as a tail is a delicacy to make a Somali mouth water or a European gorge rise.

The only serious occupation a buck Somali will permit himself is to sit under a tree and watch his grazing flocks. He is fond of conversation, chiefly of a recriminative character, and gives vent to his *joie de vivre* by prancing and singing on two or three simple notes to the accompaniment of his clapping hands and the thud of his horny heels. His chief woe is drought and lack of grazing, because he then has to get up off his butt-end and take long treks to pastures new. His ideas of earthly Paradise centre round the *cafés* of Aden, where his countrymen are numerous and where wages are so high that six grown Somalis can batten in well-fed ease on the earnings of a seventh, who keeps on till he wants a holiday and then "goes sick" and sends another of the syndicate to replace him. Qualifications do not matter, as they all have sufficient to fumble through their jobs and no more. If he lacks the capital to start cab-driving and finds boat-rowing or punkah-pulling too strenuous for him, he sets himself to learn a little English and gets a job as servant with some new-fledged British subaltern at a minimum rate of £2 a month, which is fixed by his union, for that is one civilised device he really *can* handle. He is the slackest oarsman, the laziest punkawala and the worst whip east of Suez. His idea of driving is to sit with knees drawn up toward his chin while he lugs at the reins as if they were a punkah-cord, urging his staunch little screw along with ineffectual flaps of his whip and noises like the paroxysms of sea sickness.

He will ruin any saddle-camel for fast work if allowed to ride one regularly, such animals not being raised in his country, but he breeds a small, hardy type of pony which he loves to gallop in wild dashes, with flapping legs and sawing hands, reining the poor little beast up short on a bit like a rat-trap to witch beholders with his horsemanship.

As a combatant you never know how to take him. He may put up a hefty fight or he may outrun the antelope in his precipitate retreat. I was much impressed by the defences in barbed wire and thorn trees considered necessary to ward off the onslaught of dervishes by men who knew them better than I did.

He is a cheery, irresponsible soul and has been called the Irishman of the East. Missionaries rather like him, because he is very teachable up to a certain point, fond of learning new tricks if not too difficult, and without that habit of logical and consecutive thought which makes the real Arab so difficult to tackle in argument.

No remarks on Somaliland would be complete without some mention of the Mullah. That astute personage has often been alluded to as "Mad," but has proved himself far saner than the

Government he was up against. In the early 'nineties he kept the Arabi Pasha coffee-house opposite the cab-stand in the native town at Aden, where he dispensed tea and husk-coffee in little bowls of green-glazed earthenware, also raspberryade and other bright-coloured "minerals" in bottles, with a small lump of ice thrown in. His establishment was patronised almost entirely by Somalis and largely by the *ghari-walas* themselves. At the same time, he was obliging enough to spare the servant of a neighbouring sahib like myself a pound or two of ice from his "cold box" on occasional application to meet an emergency.

He had a good deal of property in flocks and herds over in British Somaliland, which he visited from time to time. In the late 'nineties he got involved in some suit or other and the local authorities mulcted him of many camels. He very much resented this decision and raised some friends and sympathisers to resist its execution by the police. An inadequate force was sent and sustained a reverse, after which his following grew enormously. Early in this century, when I again had news of him, he had craftily cut in between the Italian, Abyssinian and British converging columns and annihilated Colonel Plunkett's gallant little band at Gumburu, but sustained a severe defeat at Jidballi, where his red flannel dressing-gown was sighted in early and headlong retirement as his dervishes recoiled from the embattled square.

All the same, he was still going strong long after the South African War was over, and we had more leisure to attend to him. When the British frontier was drawn in to enable the statement to be made in Parliament that "the Mullah's troops were no longer within protectorate limits," he took advantage of it to deal ruthlessly with those tribes which had refused to join him on the solemn and definite promise that Government would protect them from his vengeance. The unhappy Dolbahuntas were almost wiped out as a tribal unit; their zarebas and flimsy villages were surrounded by the Mullah's men and fired, leaving the occupants—men, women and children—the choice of a dreadful end among blazing thorns or red death on the spears of their fellow-countrymen and co-religionists. A prominent Nationalist has alluded to the Mullah and his dervishes as "brave men striving to be free."

In 1910 British prestige had shed its last rag in Somaliland: we had withdrawn to the coast and the Mullah's horsemen actually rode through Berbera bazar on one of their raids and withdrew unscathed. In 1912 it was found necessary to form a company of Somali police on camels to keep the peace between "friendlies" who, to allay a certain amount of indignation at home, had been armed with rifles to protect themselves against the Mullah's people, but were using these weapons, in their light-hearted way, to argue questions of grazing as they arose. Early in 1913 "a small dervish outpost" was reported to be preventing our friendlies from grazing in the Ain valley south of Burao at a time when no other pasturage was locally available, and the Somali camel-corps, about a hundred strong with three white officers, was sent to occupy Burao as its base and from there to afford moral and material support enabling the friendlies to graze unmolested in the threatened area. This cheery opportunism was the Government's wobbling attempt at equilibrium between the barefaced desertion of our protected tribes and its avowed policy of non-intervention unless on the cheap. It was done too much on the cheap; that little force was attacked by an overwhelming force of dervishes while out on the grazing grounds affording moral and material support. The Maxim was put out of action by an unlucky bullet, and the friendlies skedaddled with their Government rifles at the first shot, but returned later to loot the dead. The half-trained Somali camelry suffered severely and were most unsteady, but the two white officers surviving managed to extricate the remnant with difficulty, the gallant commandant having died for his trust early in the fight. He was blamed posthumously for having exceeded his orders; whether he ought to have exercised his moral and material support at a safe distance from the place where it was needed or have led his command in headlong flight was not made clear, and they were the only two military alternatives to the action he *did* take. At all events the incident shamed the Government into taking more adequate measures to protect its friendlies in spite of bitter Nationalist opposition.

Missionaries point to our long and fruitless struggle in Somaliland as an illustration of the force of fanaticism. It is nothing of the sort; the Mullah was a man with a grievance who was driven into outlawry by the sequence of events, and the movement was entirely political. Having once tasted the sweets of temporal power, he wanted to expand it, and used his spiritual and material influence to that end, not hesitating to order the wholesale massacre of other equally orthodox Moslems when it seemed to him politically expedient. He owed his success to his ruthless treatment of his compatriots, the difficult and scantily watered terrain, our lack of co-ordination with the Italians and Abyssinians, but above all to our parsimonious method of cadging and scraping a little money together for an expedition and stopping when the funds gave out, like a small boy with fireworks. Somaliland, with its insignificant caravan trade, its wide, waterless tracts and its sparse population of shiftless, unproductive semi-nomads, is a bad business proposition, and no Government can be blamed for hesitating to spend money on it; but if half the expenditure had been concentrated on one scheme at one time instead of being frittered away on several divergent schemes over a lengthy period the Mullah would have been brought to book and the resources of the country developed considerably.

South of Somaliland in British, and what was once German, East Africa the missionary has comparative freedom of movement, whereas in Somaliland no white man has ever been allowed to travel without the sanction of the local authorities. He, however, complains that he is not encouraged by the Administration in either colony, and certainly makes no headway against Islam, which has a very strong hold, especially in British East Africa, with the Swahilis. Still, he can point to the inland kingdom of Uganda as one of his successes, and it would be more so if the various Christian sects would refrain from wrangling among themselves.

We have now reached the southern limit of Moslem activity in Africa, for we are getting among native races who do not take kindly to asceticism in any form, and beyond them are the sturdy white Christians of South Africa. Curiously enough, there is a flourishing little colony of Moslems at Salt River, the railway suburb of Cape Town, where imported East Indian and Arab mechanics have settled. They muster about 7,000 souls and have founded a school to educate their children. An unbiassed English resident states that they are far better citizens than native Christians of the same class, owing to their temperate habits. Drink is the undoubted curse of the non-Moslem African. In South Africa no native in white employ can get alcoholic drink without the written authority of his employer, but there are many illicit sources of supply. South African colonists insist that the native Christians are the worst—this should not be set down to Christianity, but to the civilisation which goes with it, and, in place of Kaffir beer and such like home-fermented brews of comparatively mild exhilarant character, introduces the undisciplined native mind to the furious joys of trade fire-water.

Africa is the main battle-ground between Moslem and missionary, for it is in that continent that the forces of Islam and Christianity are most nearly balanced. The American Protestant Mission, which is, as we have seen, one of the principal belligerents, complains loudly on behalf of Christendom that in Africa especially our colonial administrations do not give the support to Christian missions that Christian Governments should.

Apart from the fact that we administer these countries in trust for their indigenous population and have no right to thrust our own creed upon them to the exclusion of any other with a sound system of ethics, it can most cogently be urged that Islam is the only religion which insists on total abstinence, and that seems to be the only way in which the native African can avoid alcoholic excess.

I have in front of me a letter written by an American of Boston, Mass., to the *Spectator* of February 15th, 1919. In it he alludes to a report of the Committee for preventing the demoralisation of native races by the liquor traffic which is said to be "making Africa a cesspool of alcohol, and statistics show that in this devil's work Holland with her gin and, I regret to say, the United States with its trade rum have been the conspicuously worst offenders." The writer goes on to say that the native races are morally and intellectually children, and that has been recognised in the States where it is a penal offence to introduce alcoholic drink within the Indian reservations.

This being so, the attitude of American Protestants in attacking the only teetotal creed which is working among natives in a continent where total abstinence is unanimously declared to be essential to native welfare indicates loose thinking. It is still more extraordinary when we remember that the teetotal party in the United States have moved heaven and earth and every device, legitimate or otherwise, to secure national prohibition, about which, to put it mildly, there appear to be two opinions among American citizens. We are told that the South adopted prohibition as a measure of protection against the negro. Apart from the safety of white colonists in Africa, is the welfare of African negroes beneath the consideration of a free-born American? If so, why does he (or she) subscribe so liberally to support missions in Africa? Such an attitude is incongruous, even if we adopt the preposterous view that Christianity alone can make a sober man of a negro. Imagine a municipality which allowed a gang of hooligans to scatter incendiary bombs broadcast and encouraged its inadequate fire brigade to fight a rival organisation tooth and nail. Its avowed intention of prohibiting the use of matches on its own premises would not be considered a satisfactory *amende*.

I lay no more stress on American Protestant activities against Islam than is their due. There may be some opinions among Europeans that their evangelising fervour might find a mission field nearer home in South America or even in Mexico. Such a criticism is not only ungrateful but unreasonable. American missions have done much for humanity in the East, while as regards their own sub-continent the Catholic Church has held that field for centuries, and no reasonable being wants to see the two great divisions of Christianity sparring with each other about the spiritual education of greasers.

The Monroe Doctrine does not apply to missionaries, but I would point out to them that in wrestling against Islam they are fanning the fires of fanaticism and causing much material trouble, and the net spiritual result is to lessen their own power for good and embitter Islam for ill while widening the breach between Christian and Moslem.

This chapter is an attempt to give an impartial glimpse at the relations between Moslem and missionary throughout the Eastern Hemisphere. With regard to their activities, it is neither a detailed account nor an apology. No sincere religious effort requires an apology, and if it is not sincere no apology suffices.

CHAPTER V

A PLEA FOR TOLERANCE

The world just now appears to be awaiting a millennium resulting from a concourse of more or less brilliant and assertive folk with divergent views. Presuming that the necessary change in human nature will be wrought by enactment, we have still to acquire more religious tolerance if we are to live together in unity with our Moslem fellow-subjects and neighbours.

What is the use of talking about a League of Nations and the self-decision of small States if we still seek to impose our religious views on people who do not want them and encroach on the borders of other creeds? Are other people's spiritual affairs of no account, or do we arrogate to ourselves a monopoly of such matters? Both positions are untenable.

The justification of missionary enterprise is based on Christ's last charge to His disciples: " Go ye into all the world and preach the gospel to every creature." He clearly defined that gospel as "the tidings of the kingdom," and what that kingdom was He has repeatedly told us in the Sermon on the Mount, frequent conversations with His disciples and others and the example of His daily life. He never sought to change a man's religious belief (such as it was) or his method of livelihood (however questionable it might be), but to reform him within the limits of his convictions and his duties. He has also left on record an indictment of proselytisers that will endure for all time. Of course, if the Gospel narrative is unreliable throughout (as the reverend and scholarly compiler of the "Encyclopedia Biblica" would appear to imply) then these arguments fall to the ground, but so does any possible justification of missionary enterprise. On the other hand, Moslems *do* believe and reverence the *Engîl* or Gospel, though they follow the doctrine and dogma of a later revelation.

The logical deduction from these facts is that moral training, education and charitable works among Moslems are permissible and justifiable features of missionary endeavour, if not forced upon an unwilling population, but attacks on Islam itself are not only unmerited but unauthorised and impertinent.

Many missionaries of undoubted scholarship

and breadth of view see this and model their field work accordingly, with good results; in fact, most real success in the mission field has been achieved by practical, Christian work on the above lines, and not by religious propaganda; but the flag which missionary societies flaunt before a subscribing Christian public is quite a different banner, as can be easily ascertained from their own published literature, which is very prolific and accessible to all.

In writing about Islam the authors or compilers of these works too frequently allow their zeal to involve them in a web of inconsistency and misstatement, or else they let their religious terminology take liberties with their intellect and that of the public.

We will glance briefly at their indictment of Islam as presented in their quasi-geographical works, disregarding their public utterances and tracts as privileged, like the platform-speeches and vote-catching pamphlets of a General Election; also we will keep to their own terminology and expressions as far as possible.

First and foremost, especially in the United States, where knowledge of non-Christian creeds is not so general as with us, the literature of foreign missions insists on grouping together all regions as yet unexploited by them (whether populated by heathen, Moslems, Buddhists or any other non-Christian race) and describing them indiscriminately as Gibraltars of Satan's power, a challenge to Christendom and a reproach to Zion (whatever that may mean). Yet the four great Christian Churches—Greek, Russian, Catholic and Protestant—seem powerless to check the reign of hell in Bolshevist Europe, where the liberty of man is demonstrated by murder, rapine, torture and every fiendish orgy or bestial lust which mortal mind can conceive. The people among whom these devilries are being enacted are Christians ruled by Christians, and have been Christian for centuries. They are still Christian so far as a blood-besotted clique will let them be anything. And in the face of such facts there are missionaries who enunciate in cold print that without Christianity there could be no charitable or humane organisation of any sort, or good government, or security of property, and—clinching argument—trade would suffer. Could there be any more glaring example of the cart before the horse? Does a dog wag his tail or the tail wag the dog? Is Japan hopelessly benighted and devoid of the activities described as the monopoly of Christianity? Moreover: Can Christian teaching or preaching pacify the embittered struggle between labour and capital which threatens yet to wreck civilisation? Does it even try?

There is no more ridiculous or extravagant boast among a certain class of self-appointed evangelists than the oft-repeated statement that all the modern blessings of Western civilisation are the fruit of Christianity and that the backward state of oriental Moslems is due to the absence of Christianity.

Any thoughtful schoolboy knows that it was the exploitation of coal and iron which lifted us Western nations out of the ruck, backed by the natural hardihood due to a bracing climate, otherwise the Mediterranean might still be harried by corsairs. Steam transport by land and sea was the direct offspring of these two minerals. Even then Western supremacy was gradual and only recently completed by the exploitation of petroleum, rubber and high explosives. Brown Bess, as a shooting weapon, was far inferior to the long-barrelled flint-lock of Morocco, and the Arabian match-lock could out-range any firearm in existence till sharp cutting tools made the rifle possible. What does modern surgery, or any other science of accurate manipulation, not owe to modern steel? When we turn from metallurgy to medicine, let us not forget that Avicenna was writing his pharmacopœia when

Christian apothecaries were selling potions and philtres under the sign of a stuffed crocodile.

Some exponents of Christianity would go further and arrogate to her the inception of all arts and handicrafts. Damascus blades, Cordovan leather, Moorish architecture, Persian carpets, Indian filagree, Chinese carvings and Japanese paintings all give the lie to such claims.

If we are to measure Christianity by the material progress of her adherents, what conclusions are we to draw from the history of the Roman Empire, the Byzantine Empire and the Copts? Fourteen hundred years after the birth of Christianity in Palestine the fall of Constantinople shattered her last vestige of sovereignty in the East after she had gone through centuries of decadence, debauch and intrigue such as anyone can find recorded by Gibbon or even in historical novels like "Hypatia."

Islam, to-day, is about the same age as Christianity was then, and has gone through similar stages, except that it has been spared the intrigues of an organised priesthood and its comparative frugality has protected it from oriental enervation to a certain extent.

Compared with Western Christianity its present epoch coincides with the era preceding the Reformation, when religious teaching had become stereotyped and lacked vitality, as is now the case with Moslem teaching as a rule There is no reason why Islam should not recover as Christianity did, and if it does not it will not be due to any intrinsic defect, but to its oriental environment, which has already debased and wrecked Eastern Christendom

The respective ages of the two religions induces another comparison. We are now in the fourteenth century of the Hejira ; glance at European Christendom of that period in the Christian era, or even much later, and reflect on the Sicilian Vespers, the Inquisition, the massacre of the Huguenots, the atrocious witchfinders who served that pedantic Protestant prig, James I, and all the burnings, hackings and slayings perpetrated in the name of Christendom. We must admit that no Moslems anywhere, even in the most barbarous regions, are any worse than the Christians of those days, while the vast majority are infinitely better, viewed by any general standard of humanity. Christendom's only possible defence is that civilisation has influenced Christianity for good, and not the other way about. There is one other loophole which I, for one, refuse to crawl through—that Christianity is a greater moral force than Islam or more rapid in its action. Missionaries say that Islam is incapable of high ideals owing to its impersonal and inhuman conception of the Deity, whom it does not limit by any human standards of justice. They complain that there is no fatherhood in the Moslem God; but—pursuing their own metaphor—what would an earthly father think if his acts of correction were criticised by his children from their own point of view? He might be angry, but would probably just smile, and I hope the Almighty does the same. A child thinks it most unjust to be rebuked or perhaps chastised for playing at trains with suitable noises at unsuitable seasons but it is that, and similar parental correction, which makes him become a decent member of society and not a self-centred nuisance.

Moslems shrink from applying *any* human standards to the Deity, regarding Him as the Lord of the Universe and not a popularly-elected premier. "Whatever good is from God, whatever ill from thyself," is a Koranic aphorism. Nor do they seek to drive bargains with Him, as do many pious Christians, and their supplications are limited (as in our Lord's Prayer) to the bare necessities of life—food and water to support existence, and clothing to cover their nakedness.

The application of human ideals to the Almighty places Him on a level with Kipling's "wise wood-pavement gods" or the Teutonic conception of a deity who sent the Entente bad harvests to help German submarine activities. Such absurdities incur the rebuke of the staunch old patriarch, "Though he slay me yet will I trust in him"; there is no excuse for seeking to inflict them on the austerities of Islam.

Climate and terrain have a marked influence on the form religion takes in its human manifestation. Missionary literature asserts this clearly with regard to Islam, describing it, aptly enough, as a religion of desert and oasis thence deriving its austere and sensual features, but the thesis applies with equal force to Christianity. The marked cleavage of hermit-like asceticism and gross sensuality which rock-bound deserts and the lush Nile valley wrought in Egyptian Christendom has been described by every writer dealing with that subject, and Arabian Christianity drooped, and finally died, in the arid pastoral uplands of Jauf and Nejran long before it succumbed in fertile, hard-working Yamen.

If the East became Christian next week there would be the same rank growth and final atrophy or disintegrating schism for lack of outside opposition. Missionaries are quick enough to remark on this process in Arabia where Islam is practically unopposed, but will not apply it to Christianity. They do not seem to realise that healthy competition maintains the vitality of religion no less than trade or any other form of human effort requiring continuous energy and application. Islam revivified a decadent Christianity, and the attacks of modern missionaries are strengthening Islam. They justify these attacks and urge further support for them on the grounds that Islam is moribund and now is the time to give it the *coup de grâce*, or that Islam is the most dangerous foe to Christendom in the world and must be fought to a finish lest it unite three hundred million Moslems against us. I have seen both reasons given in the same missionary book; both are absurd. The latter is a mere red herring drawn across the trail of existing facts, more so, indeed, than the ex-Kaiser's Yellow Peril, for that at least was trailed from a vast country enclosing within a ring fence a huge population of homogeneous race and creed. As for crushing Islam by missionary enterprise, you cannot kill a great religion with pin-pricks, however numerous and frequent; you can only cause superficial hurts and irritation, as in a German student's duel. Every religion contains the germs of its own destruction within itself (which it can resist indefinitely so long as it is healthy and vigorous), but no outside efforts, however overwhelming, can do aught but stiffen its adherents. The early Christian Church was driven off the face of the earth into catacombs, but emerged to rule supreme in the very city which had driven her underground; Muhammad barely escaped from Mecca with his life, but returned to make it the centre of his creed, and Crusaders died in hopeless defeat at Hattin cursing "Mahound" with their last breath as the enemy of their faith, yet their very presence there showed how Islam had revived Christianity.

Per aspera ad astra: there is no easy road or short cut to collective, spiritual progress. I am not arguing against possible "acts of grace" working on individuals, but the uplift of a race, a class or even a congregation cannot be done by a sort of spiritual legerdemain based on hypnotic suggestion. Individuals may be so swayed for the time being, and, in a few favourable cases, the initial impetus will be carried on, but most human souls are like locusts and flutter earthward when the wind drops. They may have advanced more or less, but are just as likely to be deflected or even swept back again by a change in the wind. Revivalist campaigns and salvation by a *coup de théâtre* do not encourage consecutive religious thought, which is the only stable foundation of religious belief; second-hand convictions do not wear well in the storm and sunshine of unsheltered lives, and a creed that has to be treated like an orchid is no use to anybody.

If the same amount of earnest, consecutive effort and clear thinking had been applied to religion as has gone to build up civilisation we should all be leading harmonious spiritual lives to-day and sin and sorrow would probably have been banished from the earth, but few people think of applying their mental faculties to religion, and its exploitation by modern mercantile methods is not the same thing at all. Civilisation is an accretion of countless efforts and ceaseless striving to ameliorate existing conditions, whereas religion started as a perfect thesis and has since got overgrown with human bigotry and fantasies while absorbing very little of the vast, increasing store of human knowledge. That is why civilisation has got so much in advance of religion that the latter cannot lead or guide the former, but only lags behind, like a horse hitched to a cart-tail. Missionary writers are rather apt to confuse the gifts of civilisation with the thing itself. A savage can be taught to use a rifle or an electric switch or even a flame-projecter, but this is no proof that he is really civilised. On the other hand, the scholarly recluse and philosopher whose works uplift and refine humanity may bungle even with the "fool-proof" lift which takes him up to his own eyrie in Flat-land, but he is none the less civilised.

They would have us believe that petticoats and pantaloons are the hall-mark of Christian civilisation, and one of their favourite sneers at Arabia (as a proof of its benighted condition and need of their ministrations) is "a land without manufacture where machinery is looked on as a sort of marvel." As a matter of fact, Arabia can manufacture all she really wants, and did so when we blockaded her coasts; nor is machinery any more of a marvel to the average Arabian Arab than it is to the average Occidental. Both use intelligently such machinery as they find necessary in their pursuits and occupations, though neither can make it or repair it except superficially, and both fumble more or less with unfamiliar mechanical appliances. The young man from the country blows the gas out or tries to light his cheroot at an incandescent bulb, and may be considered lucky if he does not get some swift, silent form of vehicular traffic in the small of his back when he is gaping at an electric advertisement in changing-coloured lights. It has been my object, and to a certain extent my duty, on several occasions to try to impress a party of chiefs and their retinue when visiting Aden from the wildest parts of Arabia Felix (which can be very wild indeed). On the same morning I have taken them over a man-of-war, on the musketry-range to see a Maxim at practice and down into a twelve-inch casemate when the monster was about to fire. They never turned a hair, but asked many intelligent questions and a few amusing ones, tried to cadge a rifle or two from the officer showing them the racks for small arms, condemned the Maxim for "eating cartridges too fast" and were much tickled by the gunner-officer's joke that they could have the big cannon if they would take it away with them.

These wild Arabians, when trained, make the most reliable machine-tenders in the East, as they have a *penchant* for mechanism of all sorts and will not neglect their charge when unsupervised.

We are all inclined to boast too personally of our enlightened civilisation with its marvellous mechanical appliances, but what is it after all but the specialist training of the few serving the wants of the many? If the average missionary swam ashore with an Arab fireman from a shipwreck and landed on an uninhabited island of ordinary tropical aspect, the Arab would know the knack of scaling coco-nut palms (no easy task), the vegetation which would supply him with fibre for fishing-lines and what thorns could be used to make an effective hook, while the missionary would probably be unable to get fire by friction with the aid of a bow-string and spindle.

Missionary literature is very severe on Arabia as a stiff-necked country which has hitherto discouraged evangelical activities. "Hence the low plane of Arabia morally. Slavery and concubinage and, nearly everywhere, polygamy and divorce are fearfully common and fatalism has paralysed enterprise."

This indictment is not only unjust, but it recoils on Western civilisation. Arabia is on a high enough moral plane to refuse drink, drugs and debauchery generally, while prostitution is unknown outside large centres overrun by foreigners, which are more cosmopolitan than Arab. Sanaa, which is a pure Arab city with little or no foreign element, is much more moral than London or New York. To adduce slavery and concubinage coupled with polygamy and divorce as further evidence against Arabia is crass absurdity; slaves are far better treated anywhere in Arabia than they were in the States or the West Indies; concubinage and polygamy, as practised by the patriarchs of Holy Writ, are still legal in that part of the world; there is nothing sinful about them in themselves—a Moslem might as well rebuke Western society for being addicted to whisky and bridge. He might even remind us that divorce is easier in the States than in Arabia and quote the Prophet's words on the subject: "Of all lawful acts divorce is the most hateful in the sight of God." With us a woman can be convicted of adultery in the eyes of the world on evidence that would not hang a cat for stealing cream, but in Islam the act must be proved beyond doubt by two witnesses, who are soundly flogged if their evidence breaks down, and their testimony is declared invalid for the future. This places the accusation under a heavy disability, but it is better than putting a woman's most cherished attribute at the mercy of a suborned servant or two—a far greater injustice to womanhood than bearing a fair share of a naturally hard and toilsome life, which is also a missionary complaint against Arabia. As for fatalism paralysing enterprise there, perhaps it does to a certain extent, but it cannot compare with our own organised strikes in that direction.

Another charge is that Arabia has no stable government and people go armed against each other. Tribal Arabia has the only true form of democratic government, and the Arab tribesman goes armed to make sure that it continues democratic—as many a would-be despot knows to his cost. They use these weapons to settle other disputes occasionally, but Christian cowboys still do so at times unless they have acquired grace and the barley-water habit.

These deliberate misstatements and the distortion of known facts are unworthy of the many earnest workers in recognised mission fields, and they become really mischievous when they culminate in an appeal to the general public calling for resources and *personnel* to "win Mecca for Christ," and use it and the Arabic language to disseminate Christianity and so win Arabia and, eventually, the Moslem world.

Christianity had a very good start in Arabia long before Muhammad's day, and (contrary to missionary assertion) was in existence there for centuries after his death. Not long before the dawn of Islam, Christian and pagan Arabs fought side by side to overthrow a despotic Jew king in Yamen who was trying to proselytise them with the crude but convincing contrivance of an artificial hell which cost only the firewood and labour involved and beat modern revivalist descriptions of the place to a frazzle as a means of speedy conversion—to a Jew or a cinder.

Christianity lasted in Yamen up to the tenth

century A.D. It paid tribute as a subordinate creed, like Judaism, but had far more equable charters and greater respect among Moslems. In fact, it was never driven out, but gradually merged into Islam, as is indicated by the inscriptions found on the lintel of ruined churches here and there, "There is but one God."

The published statement of a travelled missionary that the Turks stabled their cavalry horses in the ruins of Abraha's "cathedral" at Sanaa is misleading. The church which that Abyssinian general built when he came over to help the Arabs against the Jew king of proselytising tendencies has nothing left of it above ground except a bare site surrounded by a low circular wall which would perhaps accommodate the horses of a mounted patrol in bivouac. The Turks probably used it for that purpose without inquiry.

What is the use of bolstering up a presumably sincere religious movement with these puerile and mischievous statements? Apart from the rancour they excite among educated Moslems (who are more familiar with this class of literature than the writers perhaps imagine) they deceive the Christian public and place conscientious missionaries afield in a false position, for most practical mission workers know and admit that the wholesale conversion of Moslems is not a feasible proposition and that sporadic proselytes are very doubtful trophies. Knowing this, they concentrate their principal efforts on schools, hospitals and charitable relief, all based on friendly relations with the natives which have been patiently built up. These relations are jeopardised by the wild-cat utterances which are published for home consumption. If a Christian public cannot support legitimate missionary enterprise without having it camouflaged by all this spiritual swashbuckling, then it is in urgent need of evangelical ministrations itself.

Missionaries in the field have, of course, a personal view which we must not overlook, as it is entirely creditable to all parties concerned. The more strenuous forms of mission work in barbarous countries demand, and get, the highest type of human devotion and courage. It is a healthy sign that the public should support such enterprise and that men and women should be readily found to undertake it gladly. There is a great gulf between such gallantry and the calculating spirit which works from a "strategic centre," to bring about a serious political situation which others have to face.

Let us now examine the Islamic attitude toward Christianity.

The thoughtful Moslem generally admits the excellence of occidental principles and methods in the practical affairs of life, but insists that even earthly existence is made up of more than civilised amenities, economics and appliances for luxury, comfort and locomotion. It is when he comes to examine our social life that he finds us falling very short of our Christian ideals, and he argues to himself that if that is all Christianity can do for us it is not likely to do more for him, but rather less. He admits that his less civilised co-religionists in Arabia, Afghanistan, etc., lack half-tones in their personalities, which are black and white in streaks instead of blending in various shades of grey. He considers that Islam with its simple austerities is better suited to such characters than Christianity with its unattainable ideals. He himself has visited Western cities and observed their conditions shrewdly. He regards missionaries as zealous bagmen travelling with excellent samples for a chaotic firm which does not stock the goods they are trying to push. The missionary may say that he has no "call" to reform existing conditions in his own country, just as the bagman may disclaim responsibility for his firm's slackness; but such excuses book no orders. The travelled Moslem will shake his head and say that he has seen the firm's showrooms, and their principal lines appeared to be Labour trouble, profiteering and diluted Bolshevism, with a particularly tawdry fabric of party politics. He respects the spiritual commercial traveller and his opinions, if sincere (he is a judge of sincerity, being rather a casuist himself), but wherever he has observed the workings of Christianity in bulk it has not had the elevating and transcendental effect which it is said to have; that is, he has not found the goods up to sample and will have none of them.

He seldom realises (to conclude our commercial metaphor) that most Christian folk in countries which export missionaries are born with life-members' tickets entitling them to sound, durable goods which are not displayed in our spiritual shop-windows or in the missionary hand-bag:—the prayers of childhood and the mother's hymn, the distant bells of a Sabbath country-side, the bird-chorus of Spring emphasising the magic hush of Communion on Easter morning, the holly-decked church ringing with the glad carols of Christmastide and the tremendous promise which bids us hope at the graveside of our earthly love. It is such memories as these, and not the stentorian eloquence of some popular salvation-monger in an atmosphere of over-crowded humanity, which go to make staunch Christian souls.

The possible proselyte from Islam has to rely on what the missionary has in his bag. Large quantities of faith are pressed upon him which do not quite meet his requirements, as it is his reason which should be satisfied first; no one can believe without a basis of belief.

There is also a great deal of slaughter-house metaphor which does not appeal to him at all, as he looks on blood as a defilement and a sheep as the silliest animal in existence—except a lamb. These metaphors were used by our Lord in speaking to a people who readily understood them, but for some obscure reason they have not only been retained but amplified extensively to the exclusion of much beautiful imagery which is still apposite. We Christians reverence such similes for their associations, but a Moslem misses the point of them, just as we miss the stately metre of the Koran in translation.

The would-be convert from Islam must, of course, learn to stifle any fond memories of the virile, vivid creed he is invited to renounce. No longer must he give ear to the far-flung call proclaiming from lofty minarets the unity of God and the Prophet's mission or its cheery, swinging reiteration as the dead are carried to the *magenna* or "gate of Heaven." Certainly not; the less he contemplates their fate the better for his peace of mind, since (if the effort to convert him is anything more than an outrageous piece of impudence) their lot in the hereafter must be appalling and his own depends on the thoroughness with which he steels his heart against all he ever knew and loved before he met that pious man and his little picture pamphlets.

Do proselytising missionaries in the Islamic field ever sit down and think what they are really trying to do? Does the social ostracism of a human being, the damnation of his folk and the salvation of none but a remnant of mankind mean anything to them? If so they ought to be overcome with horror—unless it is their idea of humour, which I cannot believe.

To pester a man into abandoning a perfectly sound and satisfying religion for one which may not suit him so well is more reprehensible than badgering a man to go to your doctor when his own physician understands his case and has studied it for a long time. At least his discarded medical adviser will not make his life a burden to him—a burden which the proselytiser does not have to share.

On the other hand, Moslems are often glad enough to avail themselves of such Christian works as mission education, medical treatment and organised charity, so they should tolerate the proselytising propaganda which seems inseparable from these enterprises.

Missionaries afield are usually justified by their works; it is the aggressive policy blazoned abroad from mission headquarters which does so much mischief. Islam was never intended to overthrow Christianity, but to bring back pagan Arabs to the true worship of God. Mission policy clamours for attack on it as if it were an invention of the devil and then complains of Moslem fanaticism, forgetting that if it were an artifice of Satan they cast doubts on the omnipotence, omniscience or beneficence of God for permitting it to exist and flourish. Otherwise, they infer that they are in a position to correct the Almighty in this matter. It is their complacent pedagogy which exasperates Moslems so. It is not the way to treat people who believe in the Immaculate Conception, who call Christmas Day "*the* Birthday" and respect us as "People of the Book."

It is time some protest was lodged against this policy if only on behalf of Christian administrations in Moslem countries, which are always being attacked by it and urged to give more facilities of spiritual aggression, especially just at present when Turkey's power has been shattered and mission strategy thinks it sees an opening.

There was never a less desirable moment for unchecked religious exploitation than now, when the war-worn nations of Christendom are trying to reconstruct themselves, and the world is seething with unrest and overstocked with discarded weapons of precision.

There is no compromise in religion, nor should there be; you cannot go halfway in any faith, and no one wants a mongrel strain begotten of the two great militant creeds such as our leading exponent of paradox wittily describes as "Chrislam." Yet surely there is a reasonable basis for a religious *entente* between Islam and Christianity.

Think what Islam has done to advance the knowledge of humanity long before the dawn of modern science. Moslems, too, would do well to remember what Christian civilisation has done for them in trade, agriculture and industries. If you accept gifts from others you should tolerate their ways; it is but an ill-conditioned cur that bolts the food proffered and then snarls.

A Moslem or a Christian worthy of the name will remain so. He may expand or (more rarely) contract his views, but will still be a Moslem or a Christian, as the case may be.

No human being has the right to say that his conception of the Deity is correct and all others wrong, nor is such a conclusion supported by the Gospel or the Koran.

It is the alchemy of the human soul which can transmute the dross of a sordid environment to the gold of self-sacrifice, and the gold of inspired religion to the dross of bigotry.

Whether we believe, as Christians, that Christ died on the Cross and rose the third day, or, as Moslems, that He escaped that fate by an equally stupendous miracle, we know that He faced persecution and death for mankind and His ideals, and that both creeds are based on the same great doctrine—" God is a Spirit: and they that worship him must worship him in spirit and in truth."

FINIS